FishFace

rtraits by David Doubilet

Fish hate to have their picture taken. They dislike it even more than cats, birds, wild orang-utans or two-year-olds – a fish portraitist is an underwater oxymoron. It is virtually impossible to be a Karsh of the coral reef. Exquisite photographic moments in the sea are even more rare than those on land, and time underwater is constantly constrained by physics and physiology.

For humans, fish appear as alien creatures living in a weightless twilight world. For fish, human divers appear to be not just aliens but true monsters with giant blank, masked eyes and Medusa-like pipes sprouting from their heads, making violent bubbling noises.

When we do meet it is fleeting, but at times we are face to face, and I am looking into extraordinary turret eyes that see 180 degrees on each side of the fish's face. Then there are small moments when suddenly there seems to be an expression.

Fish are caricatures of humans – floating cartoons. Groupers look like everybody's Uncle Max and should be smoking cigars. Parrot fish, with their protruding teeth, all seem to be named Lou. The Red velvet fish from Tasmania has a swept back dorsal fin that resembles a pompadour, giving it an Elvis-like look. The Elephant fish looks like Eleanor Roosevelt or Margaret Thatcher.

There are crustaceans and turtles in this book as well as fish. I have included them because they share the same wonderful weightless expressions that fish have. And the variety is endless – from the nightmare-like faces of the Stargazer, to endearing faces like that of the Harlequin tusk fish with its tiny, bright blue, tusk-like teeth.

Most fish pictures show fish swimming away into the blue, but for a moment, in this book, they look at us.

David Doubilet

Red-lipped Caribbean bat fish, Isle of Youth, Cuba, 2000

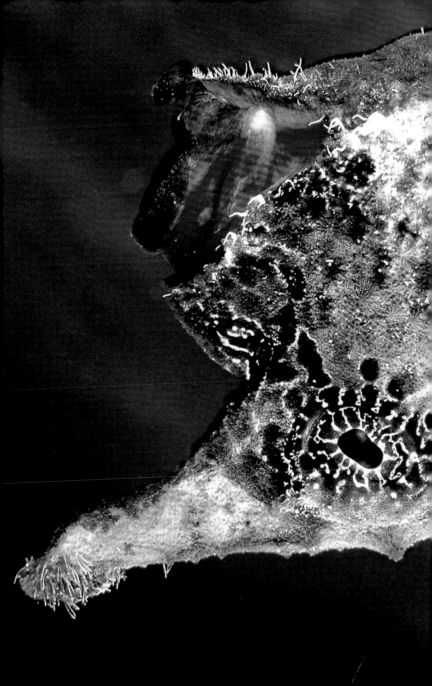

Cookie cutter shark, Suruga Bay, Japan, 1979

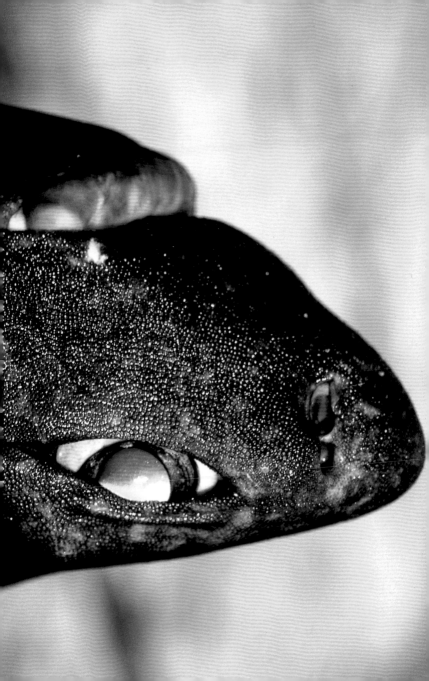

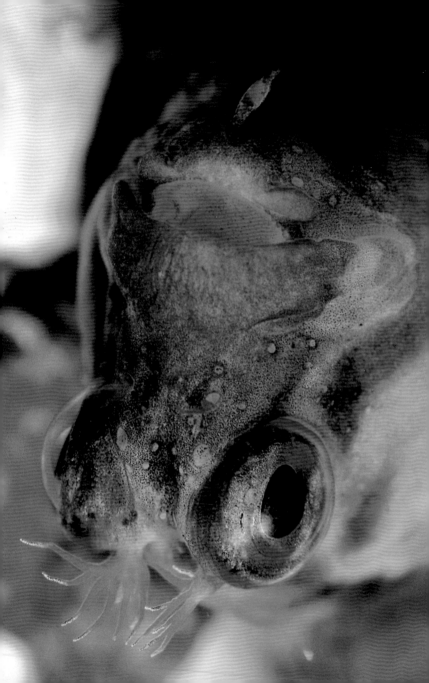

Blenny, Poor Knights Islands, New Zealand, 1987
Overleaf: Black cod and shipwreck, Middleton Reef,
Australia, 1987

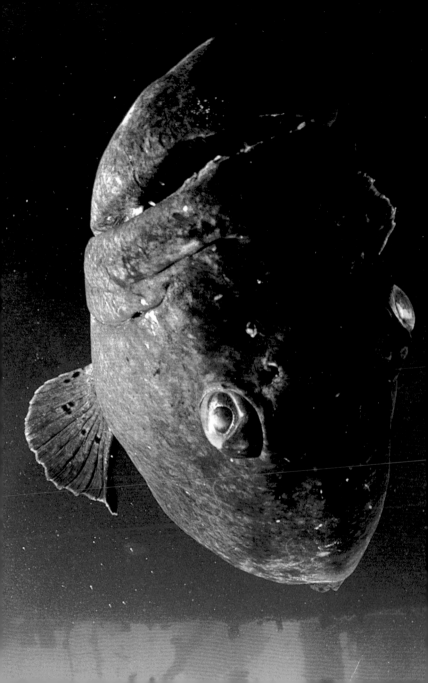

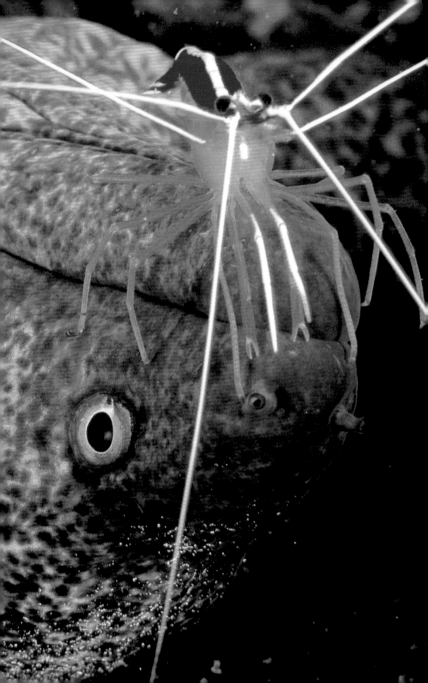

Yellowmargin moray eel and Cleaner shrimp,
Mabul, Malaysia, 1996
Overleaf: Bumphead wrasse, Red Sea, Israel, 1980

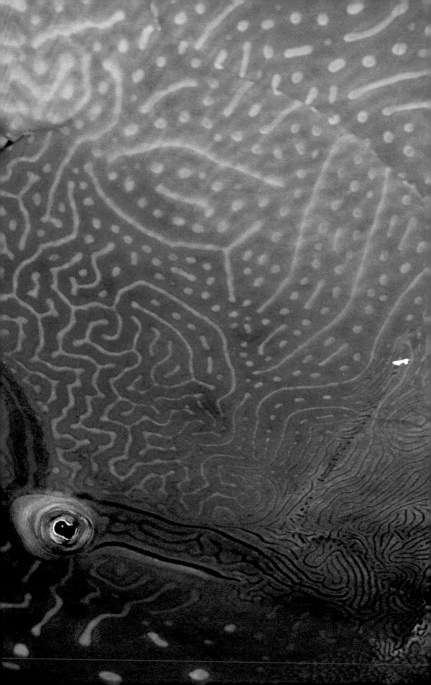

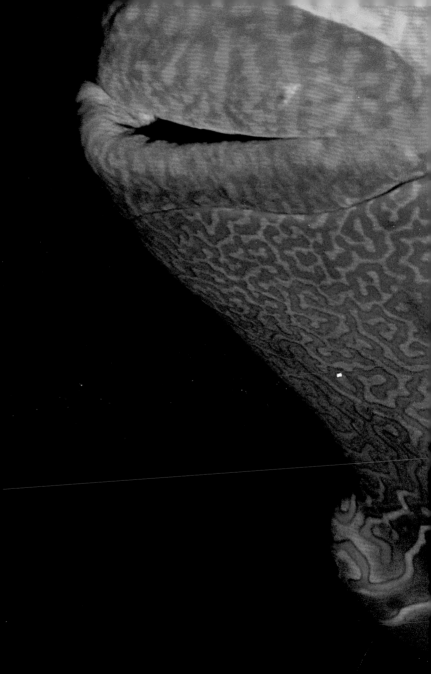

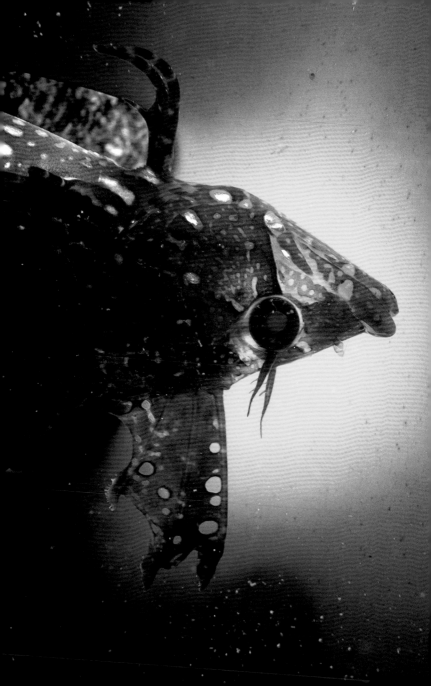

Long-nosed weed fish, Tasmania, Australia, 1995
Overleaf: Porcupine fish, Red Sea, Israel, 1982

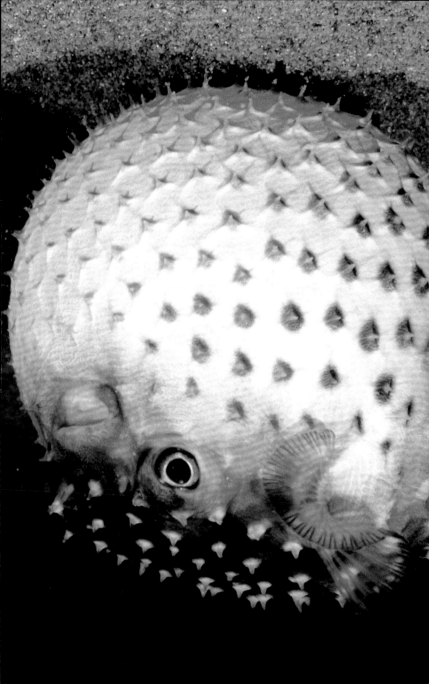

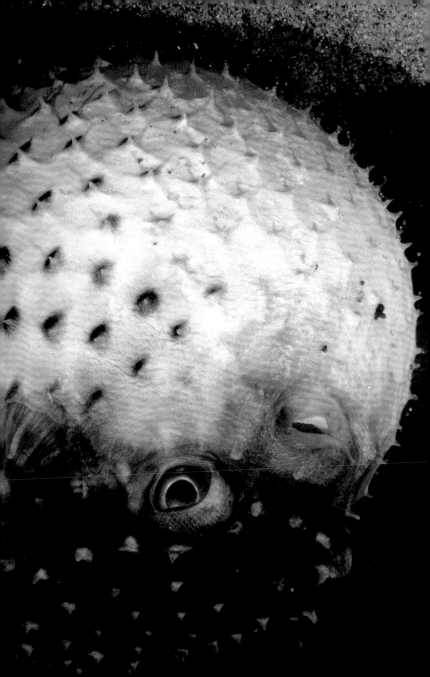

Yellow puffer fish, Aldabra Atoll, Seychelles, 1993

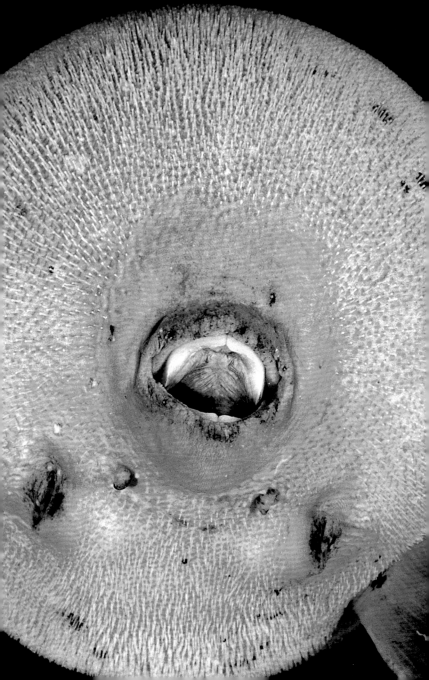

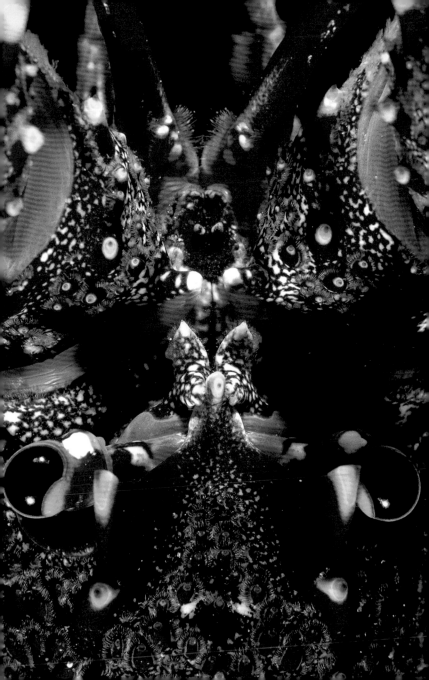

New Zealand rock lobster, Doubtful Sound,
New Zealand, 1986

Saw shark, Tasmania, Australia, 1995

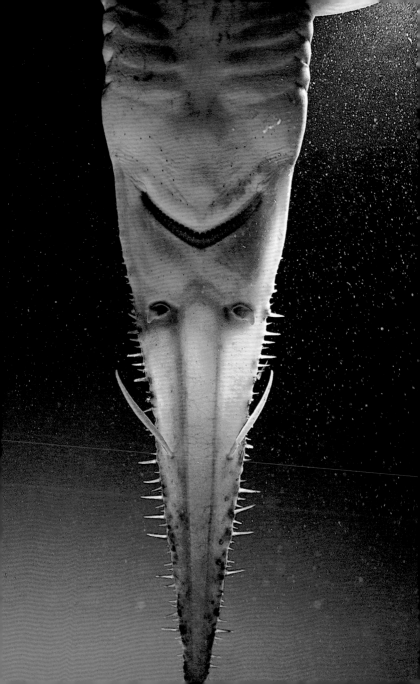

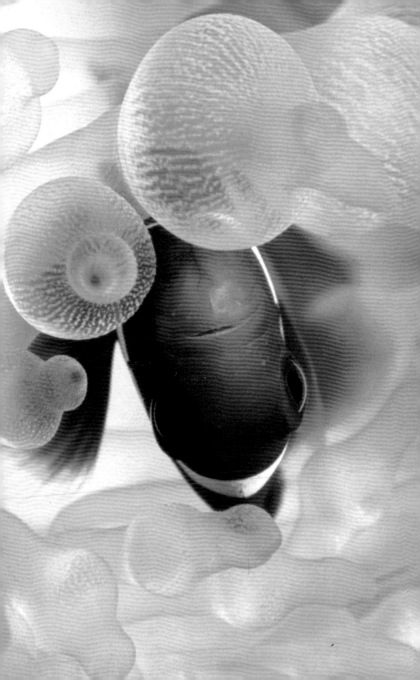

Spine-cheeked anemone fish, Kimbe Bay,
Papua New Guinea, 1997

Red and black anemone fish, Milne Bay,
Papua New Guinea, 1997

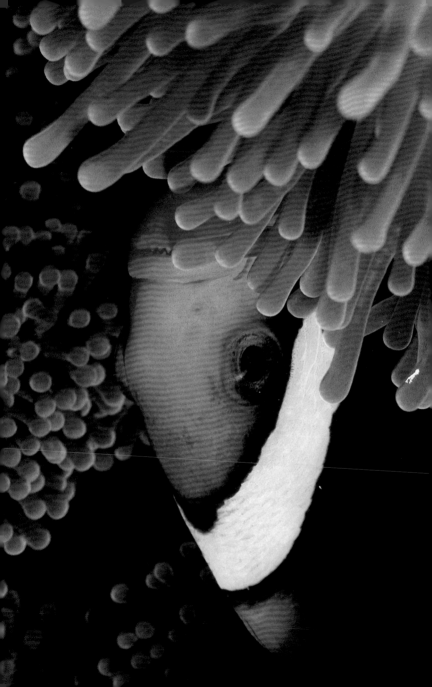

Great barracuda, Little Cayman Island, 1999

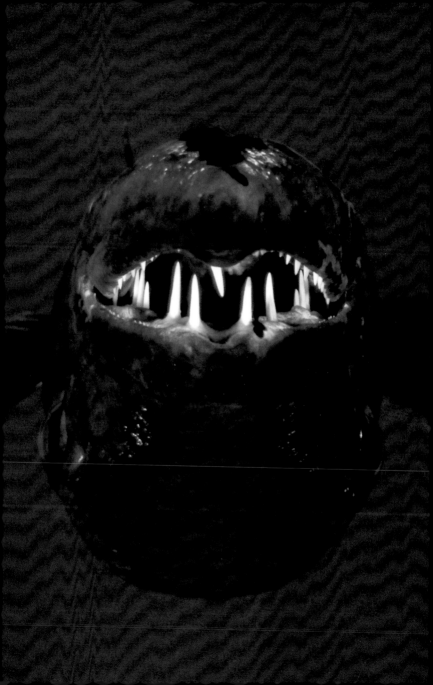

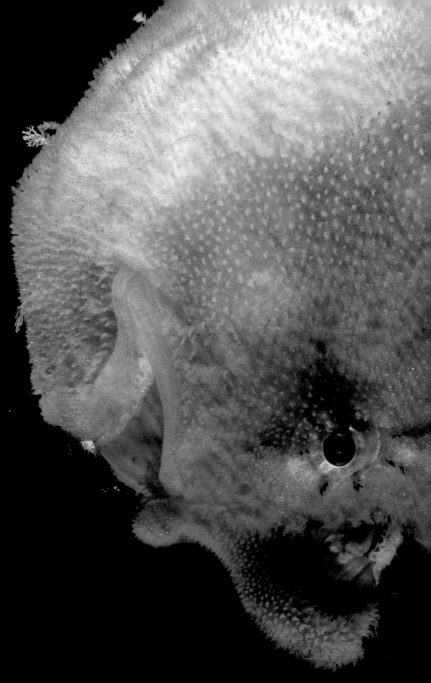

Yellow angler fish, Izu, Japan, 1989
Overleaf: Bicolour parrot fish, Red Sea, Egypt, 1991

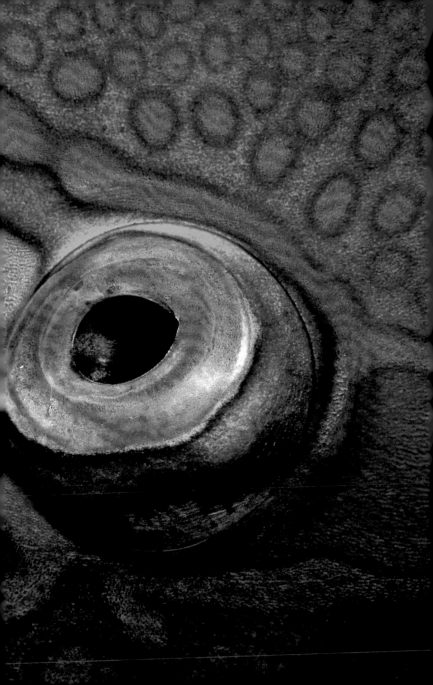

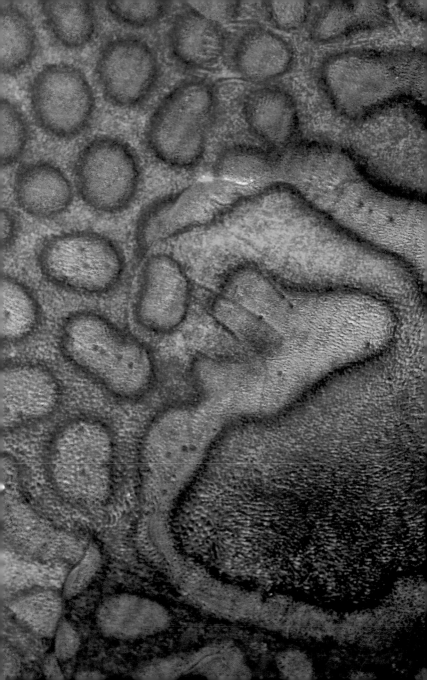

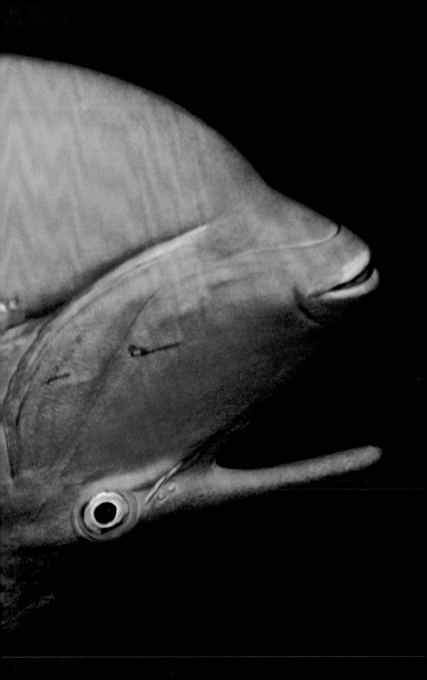

37

Unicorn fish, Red Sea, Israel, 1974
Overleaf: Blue-barred parrot fish, Sipadan Island,
Malaysia, 1997

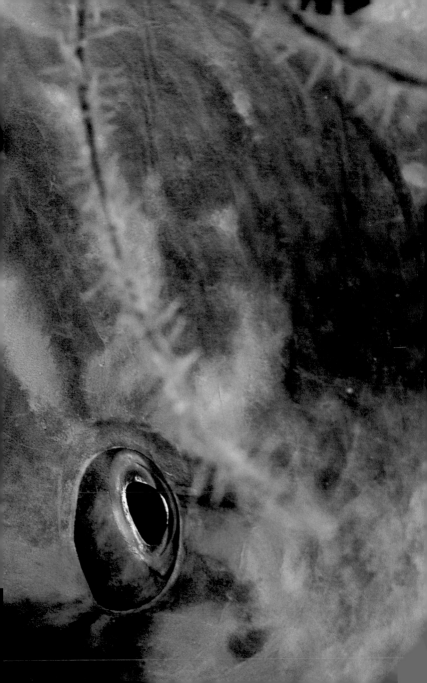

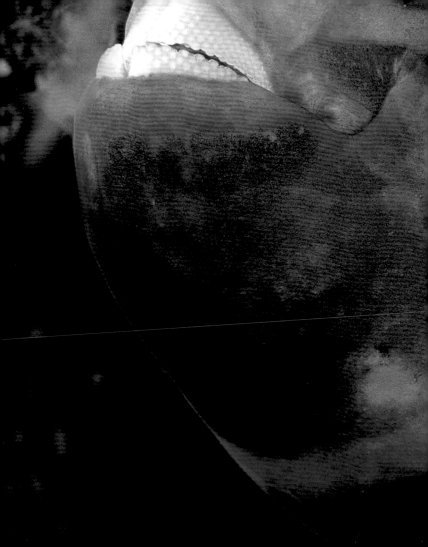

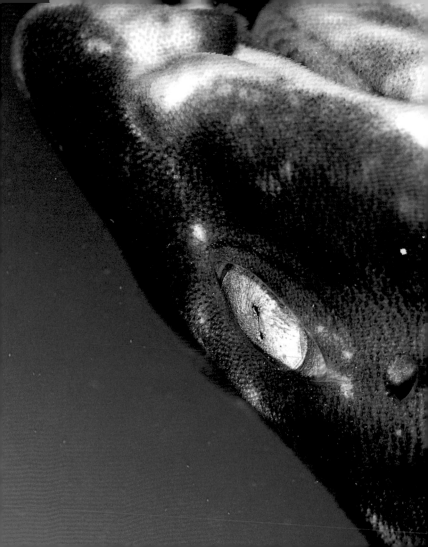

Swell shark, Channel Islands, California, USA, 1996
Overleaf: Silky shark, Gardens of the Queen, Cuba, 2000

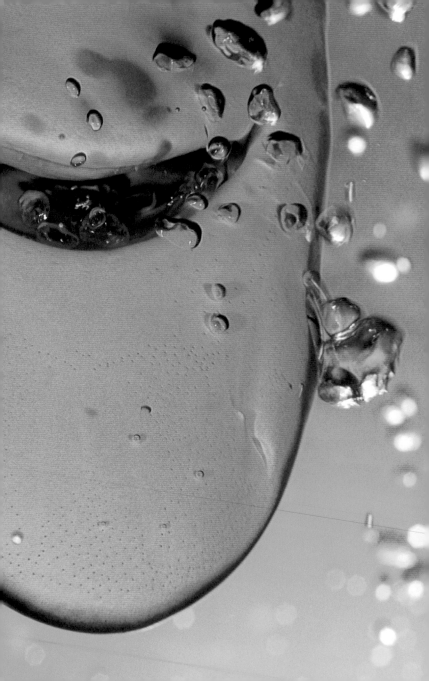

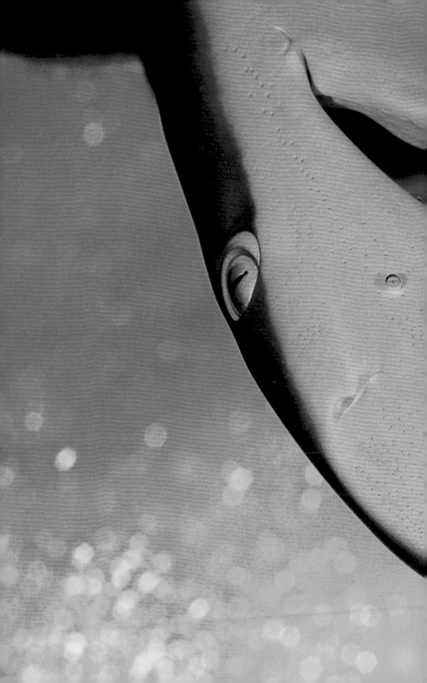

Midas blenny, Red Sea, Israel, 1985

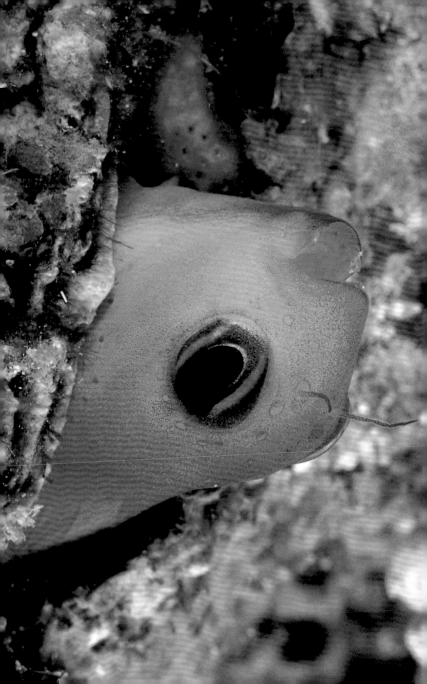

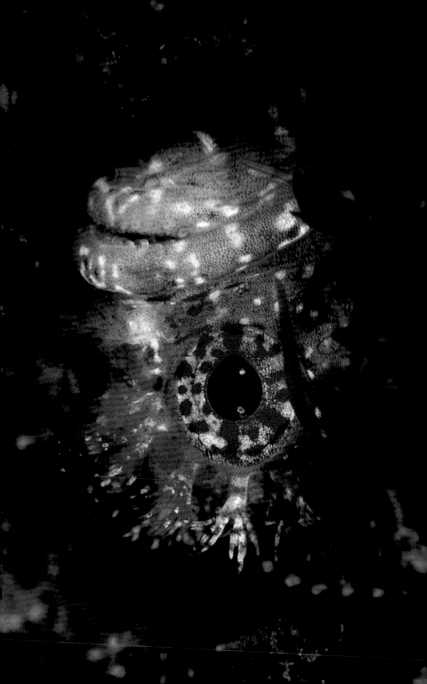

Fringehead blenny, Izu, Japan, 1981
Overleaf: Crocodile fish, Yap Island, Micronesia, 1992

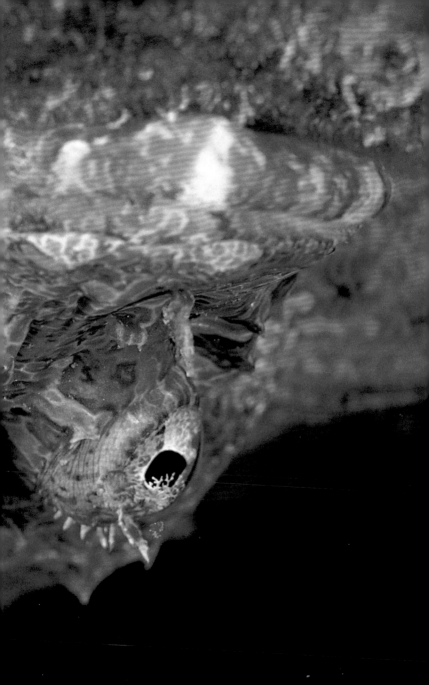

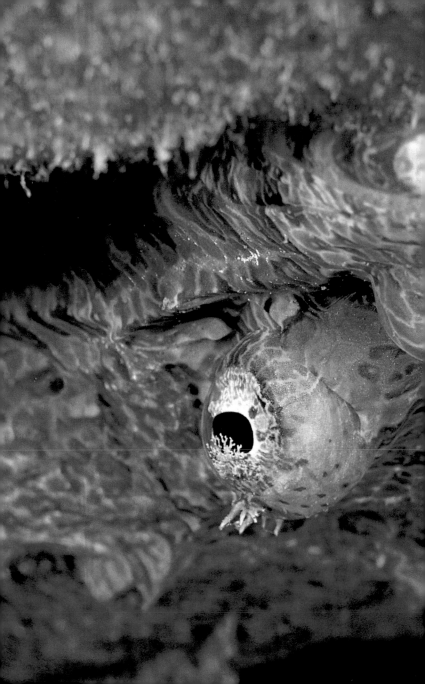

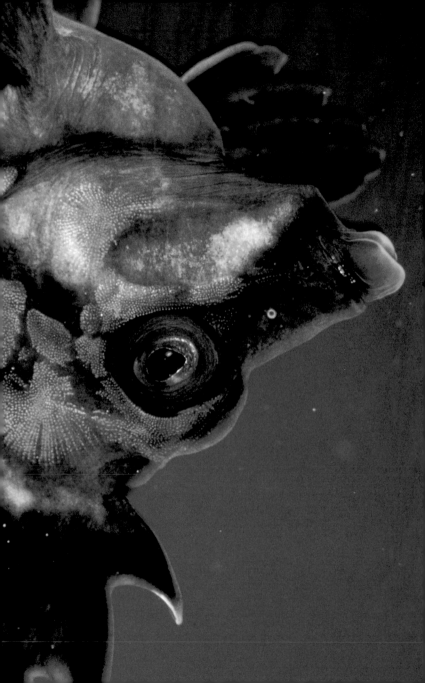

51

Pig fish, Stewart Island, New Zealand, 1987
Overleaf: Diagonal-banded sweetlips and Cleaner
wrasse, Great Barrier Reef, Australia, 1999

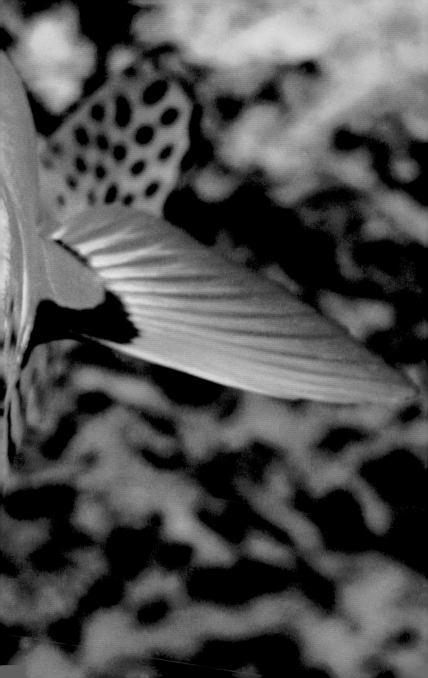

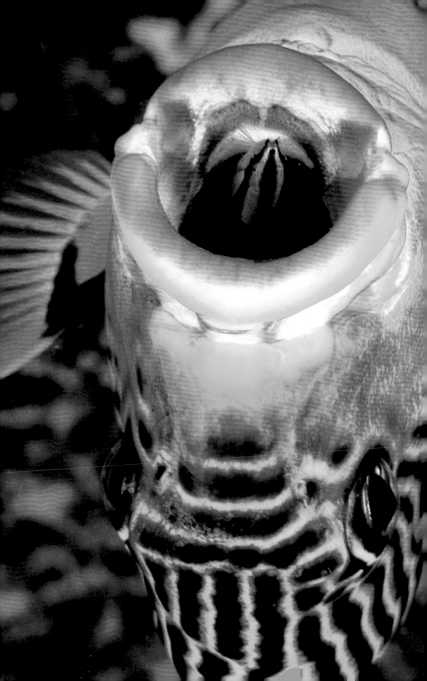

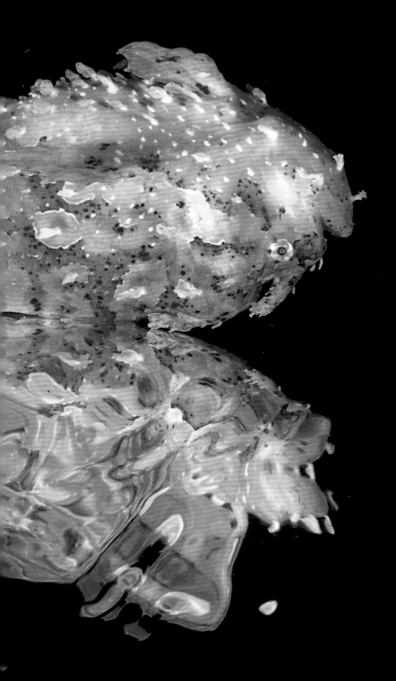

Sargassum angler fish, Kungkungan Bay,
Indonesia, 2001
Overleaf: Tomato grouper, Kimbe Bay,
Papua New Guinea, 1997

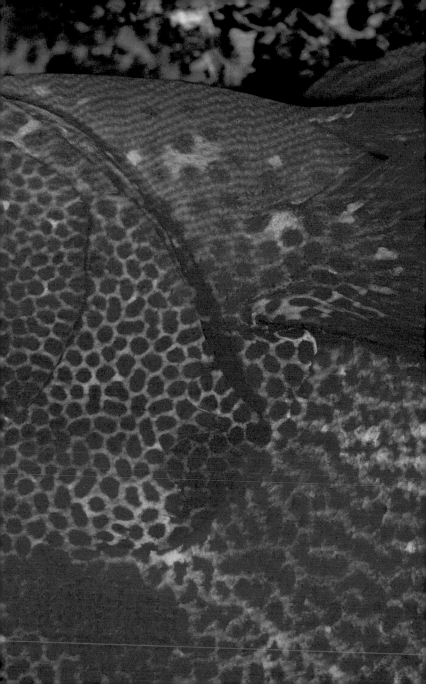

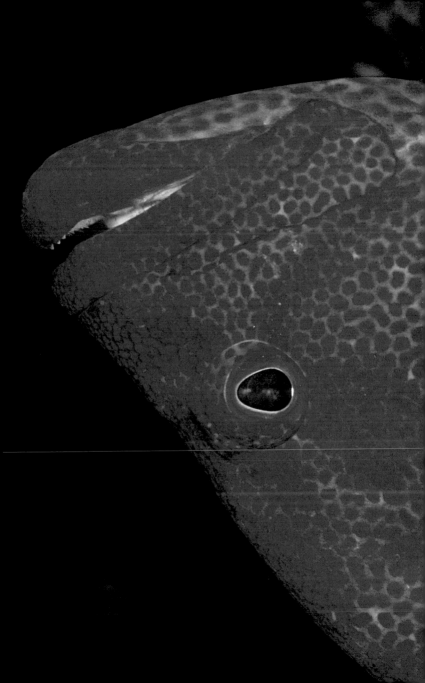

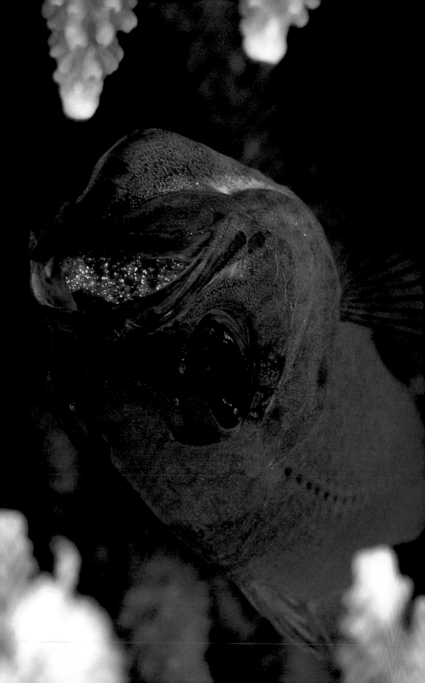

Narrow-lined cardinal fish, Bali, Indonesia, 1997
Overleaf: Puffer fish, Aldabra Atoll, Seychelles, 1992

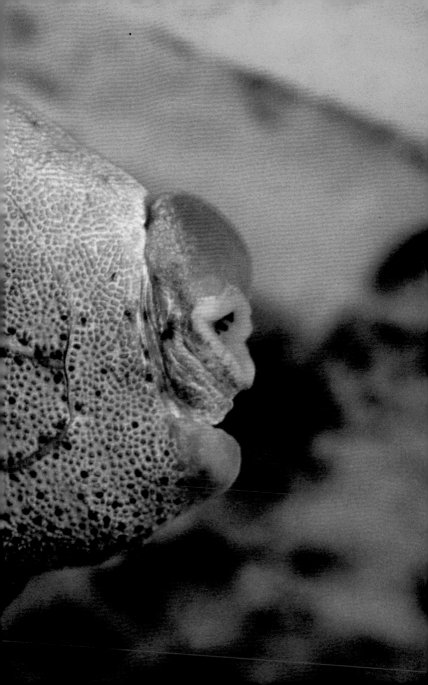

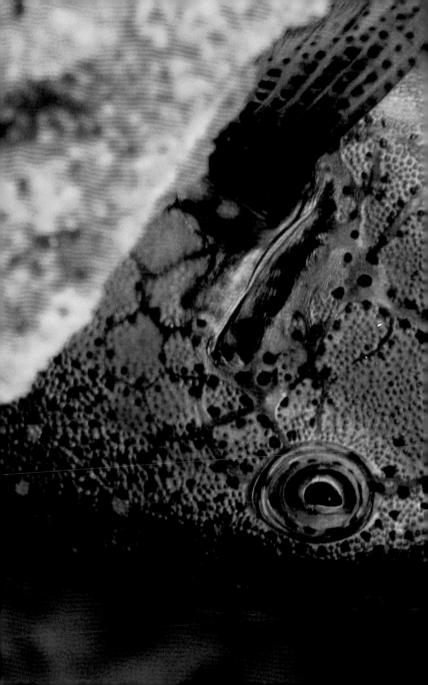

Earspot angel fish, Aldabra Atoll, Seychelles, 1993

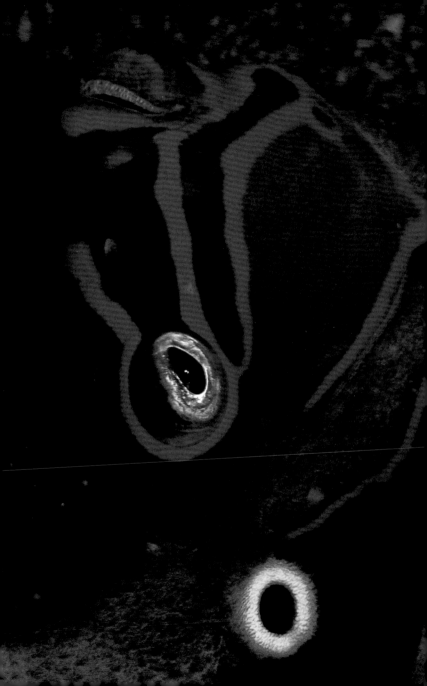

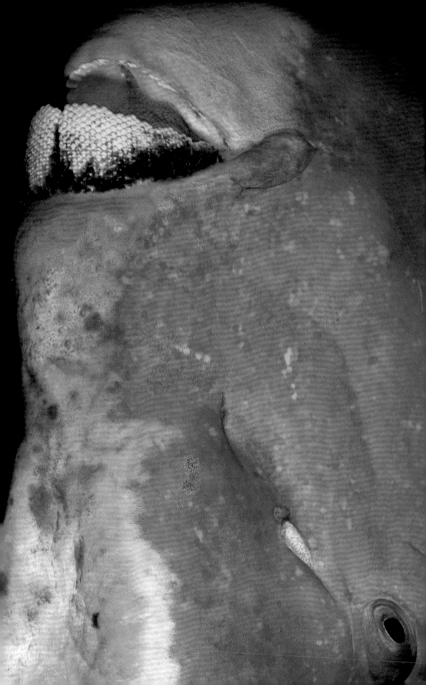

Bumphead parrot fish, Sipadan Island, Malaysia, 1997
Overleaf: Bumphead parrot fish, Sipadan Island,
Malaysia, 1997

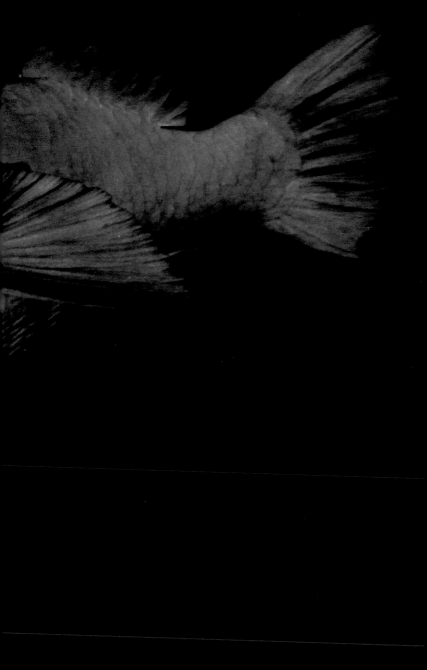

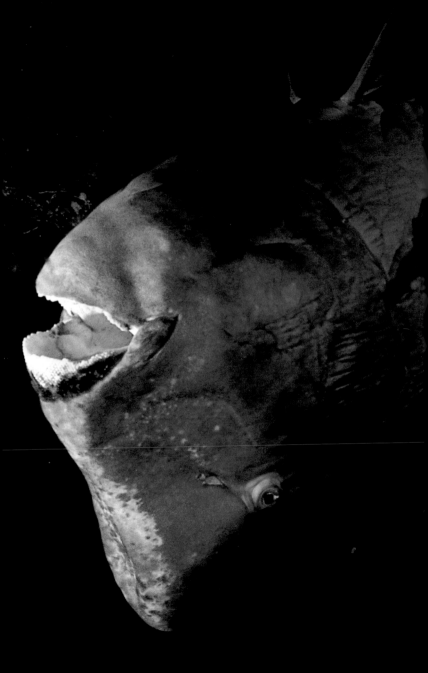

Blue-spotted grouper and Cleaner wrasse,
Great Barrier Reef, Australia, 1989

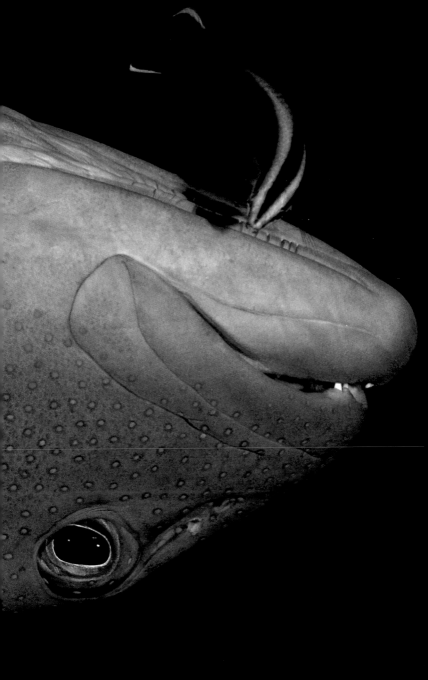

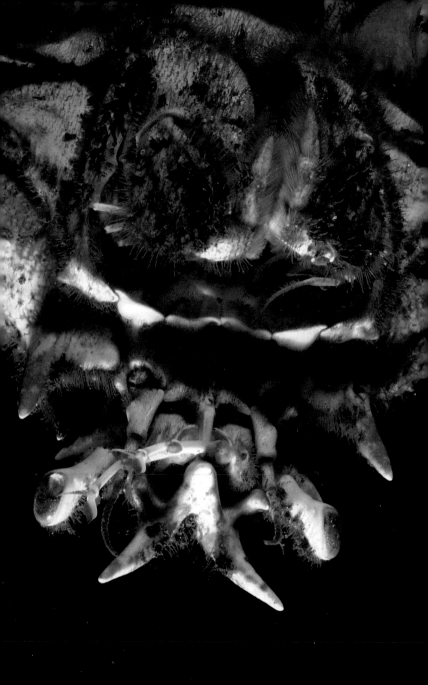

Giant Japanese spider crab, Izu, Japan, 1989
Overleaf: Hermit crab, Cayo Largo, Cuba, 2000

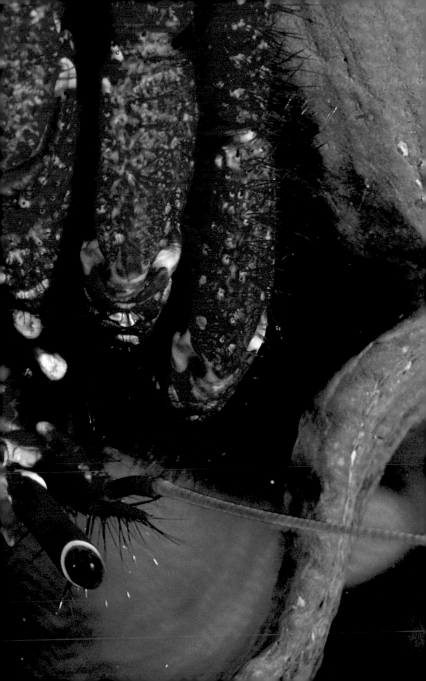

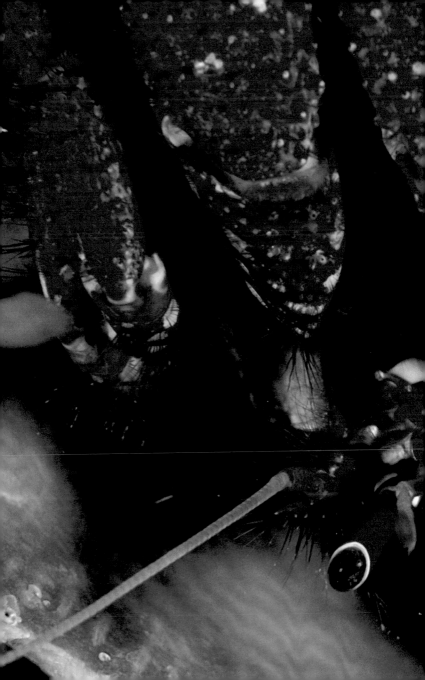

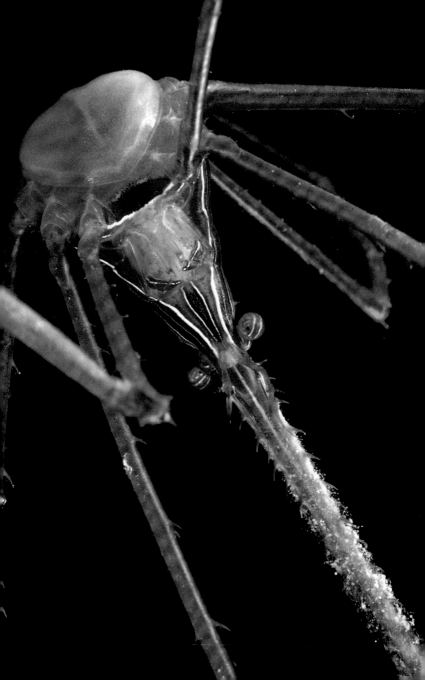

Arrow crab, Grand Cayman Island, 1984
Overleaf: Wolf eel, Vancouver Island, Canada, 1979

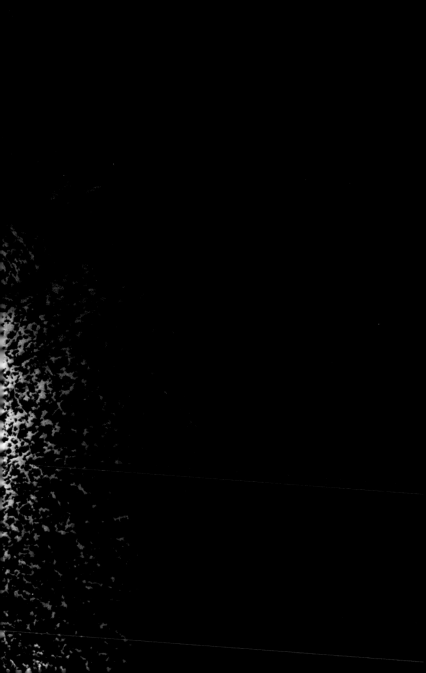

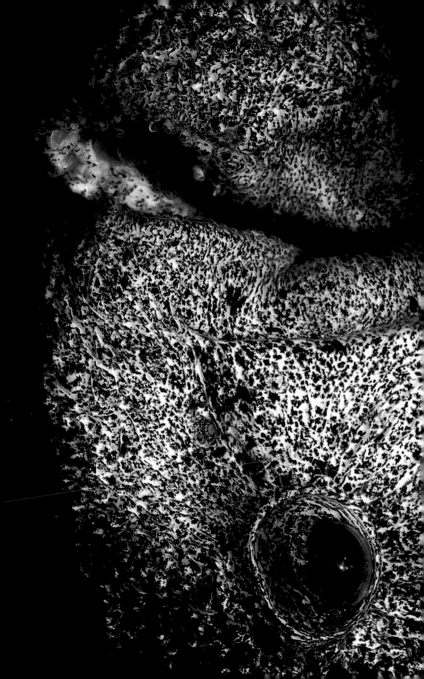

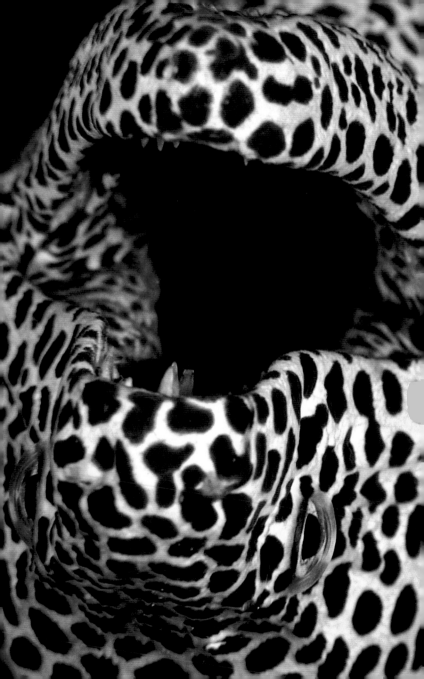

Black-spotted moray eel, Djibouti, East Africa, 1992
Overleaf: Japanese tora (tiger) moray eel, Izu,
Japan, 1984

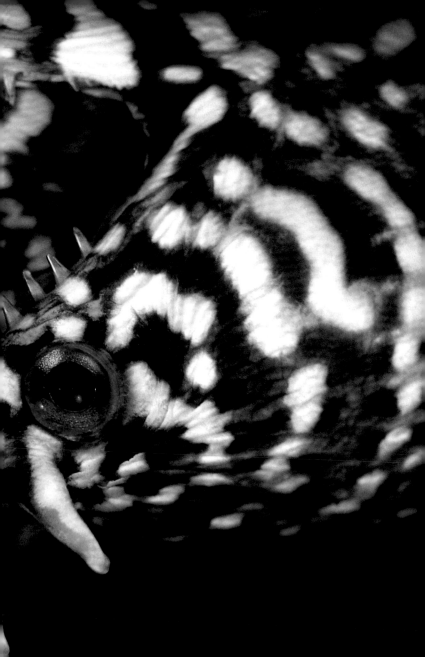

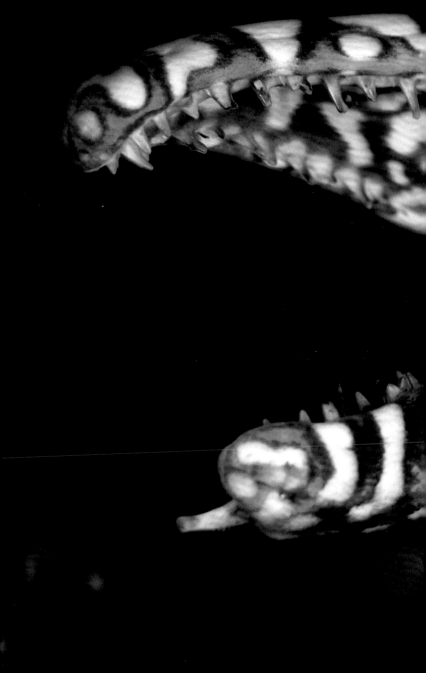

Juvenile emperor angel fish, Red Sea, Israel, 1985

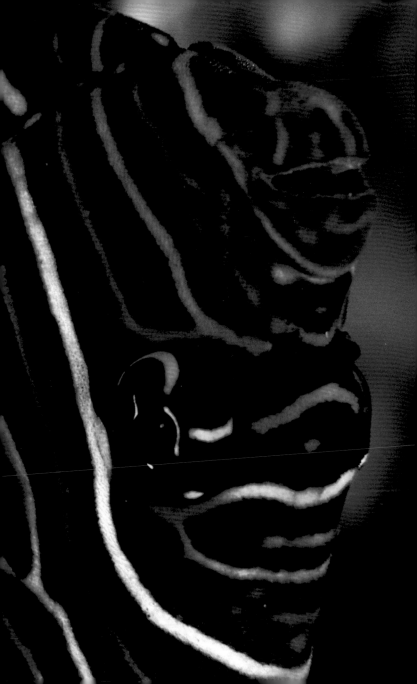

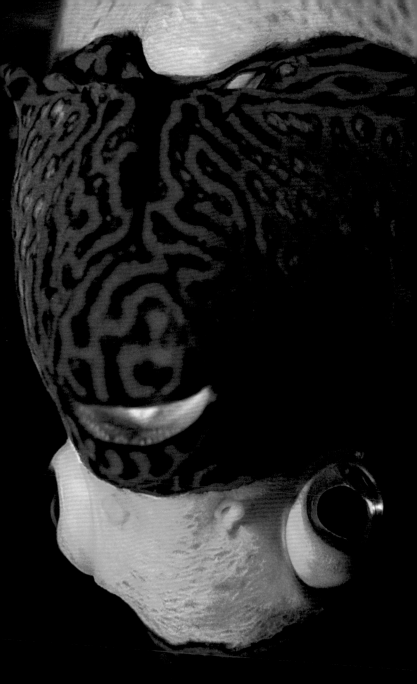

Yellow-masked angel fish, New Ireland,
Papua New Guinea, 1987
Overleaf: Mantis shrimp, Bali, Indonesia, 1997

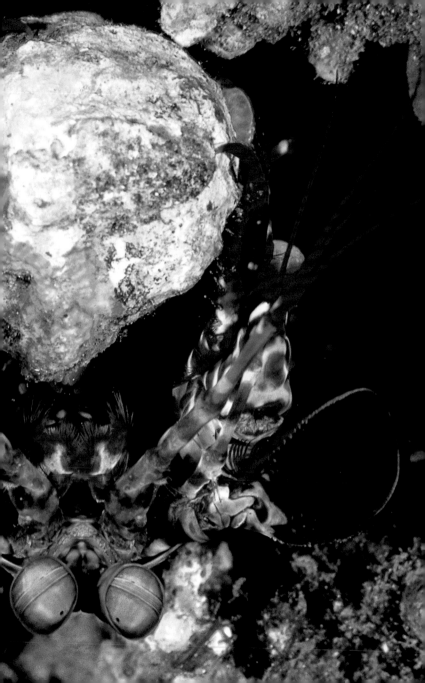

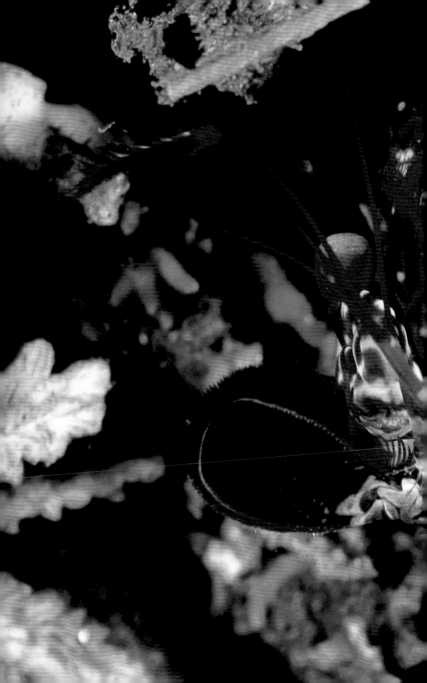

Female Tasmanian king crab, Australia, 1995

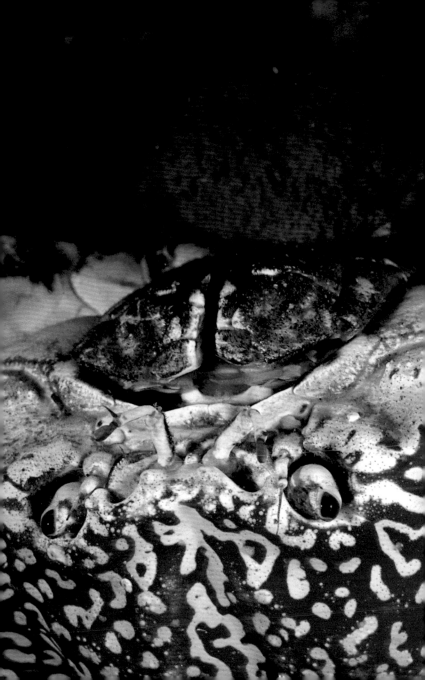

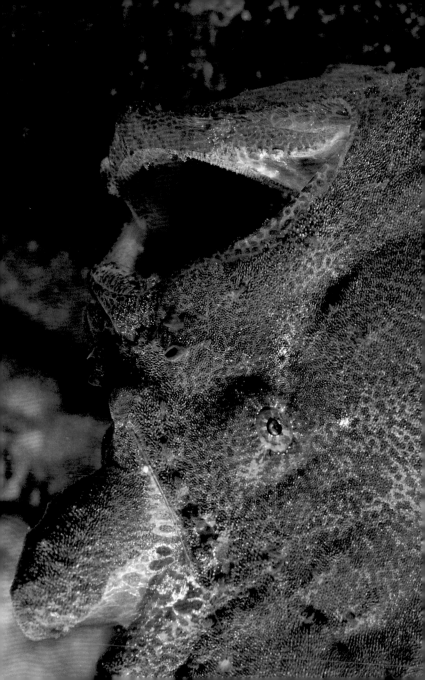

Potato-faced angler fish, Kungkungan Bay,
Indonesia, 2001

Yellow hairy angler fish, Milne Bay,
Papua New Guinea, 1994

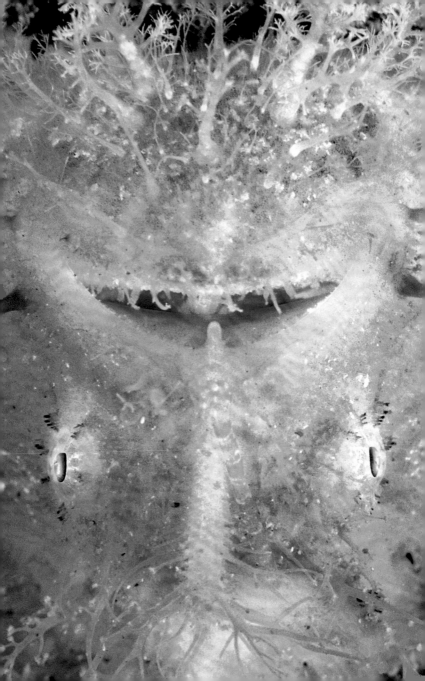

Spotted snake eel, Suruga Bay, Japan, 1989

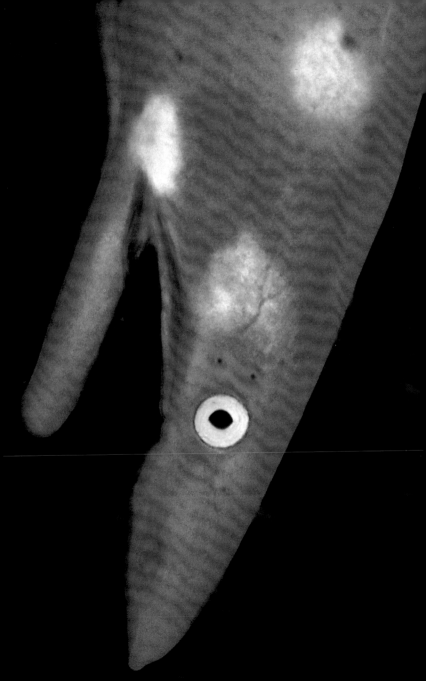

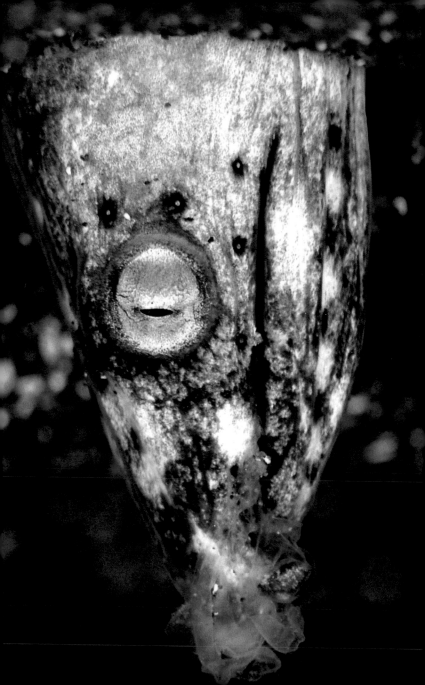

Snake eel, Suruga Bay, Japan, 1989
Overleaf: Pacific moray eel and Red shrimp,
Channel Islands, California, USA, 1985

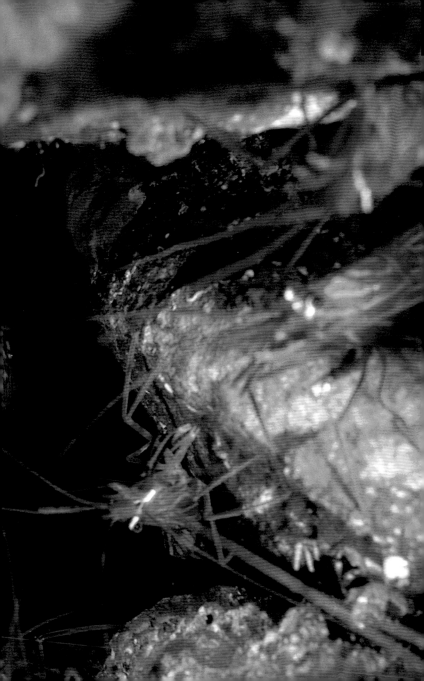

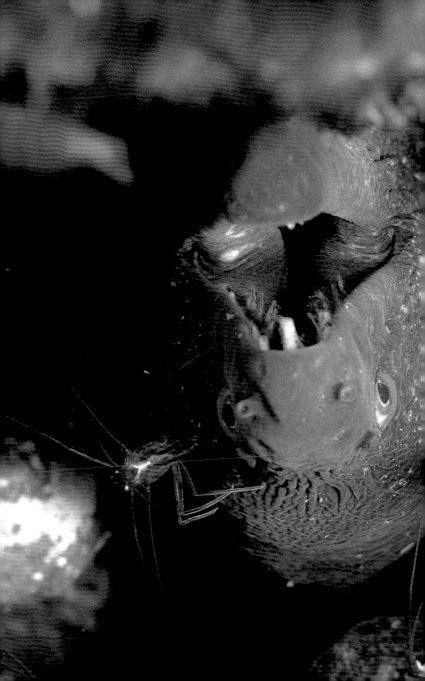

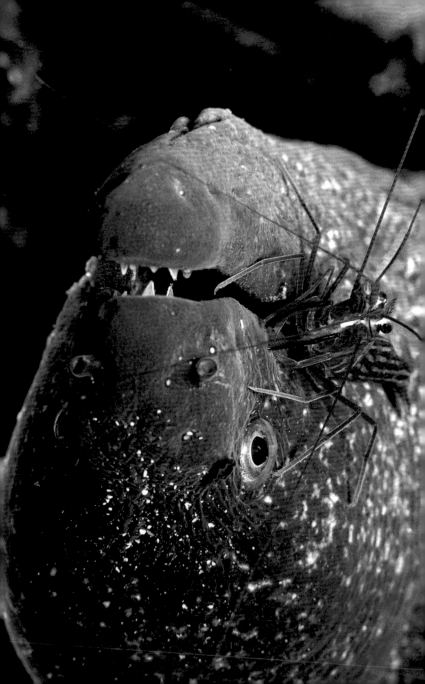

Pacific moray eel and Red shrimp, Channel Islands,
California, USA, 1985

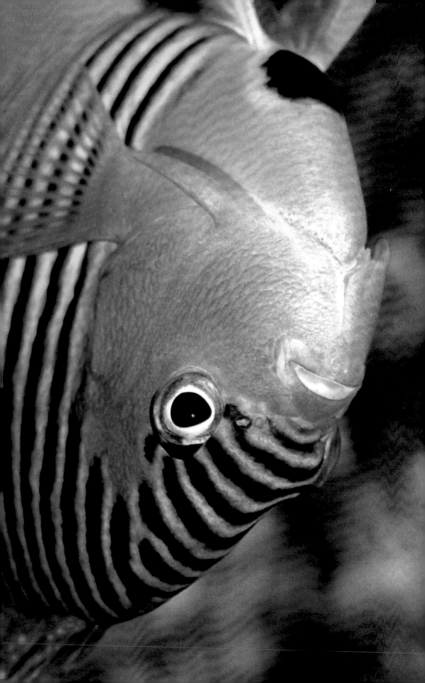

Blackspot angel fish, Kimbe Bay,
Papua New Guinea, 1996
Overleaf: Blue ribbon eel, Milne Bay,
Papua New Guinea, 1994

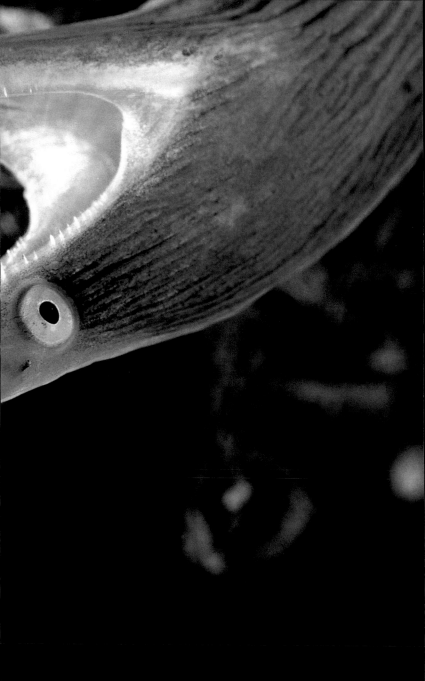

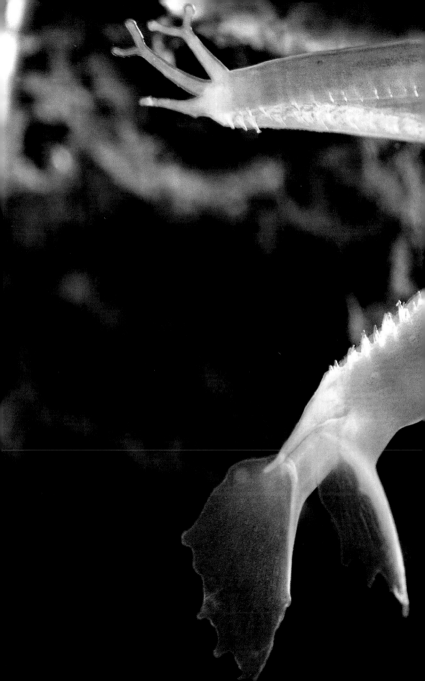

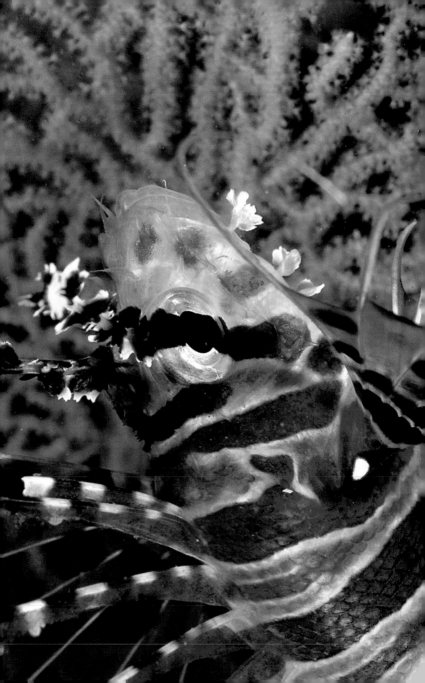

Zebra lion fish, Flores, Indonesia, 1997
Overleaf: Wolf eel and Sea urchin, Vancouver Island,
Canada, 1980

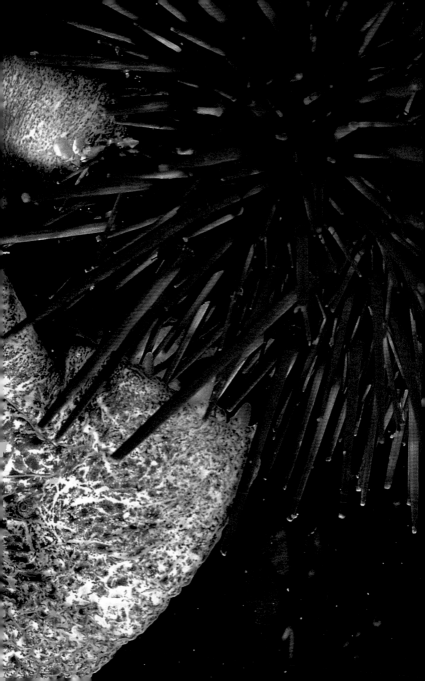

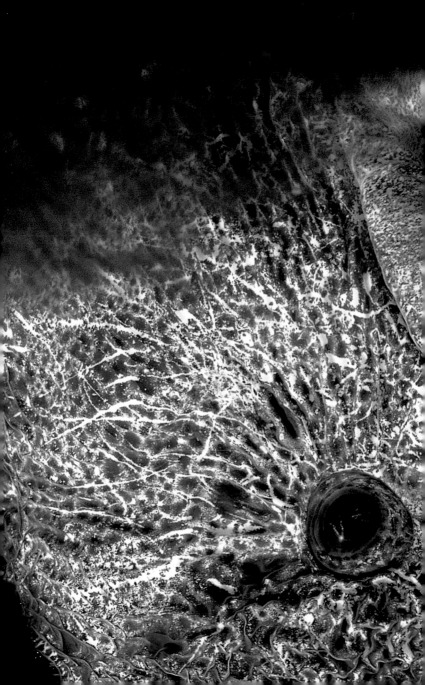

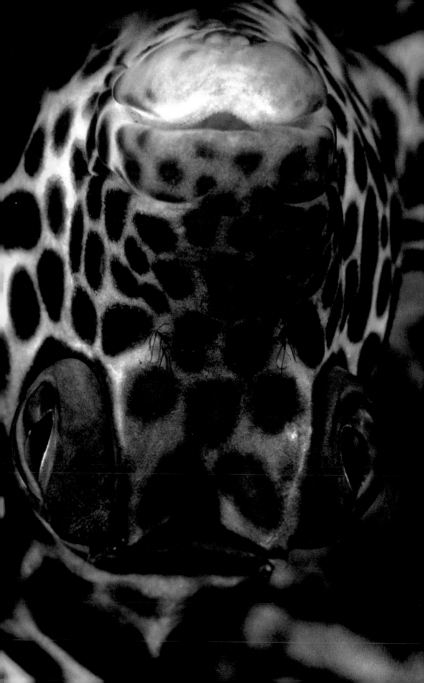

Lord Howe Island hawk fish, Australia, 1987
Overleaf: White-eyed moray eels, Shark Bay,
Western Australia, 1989

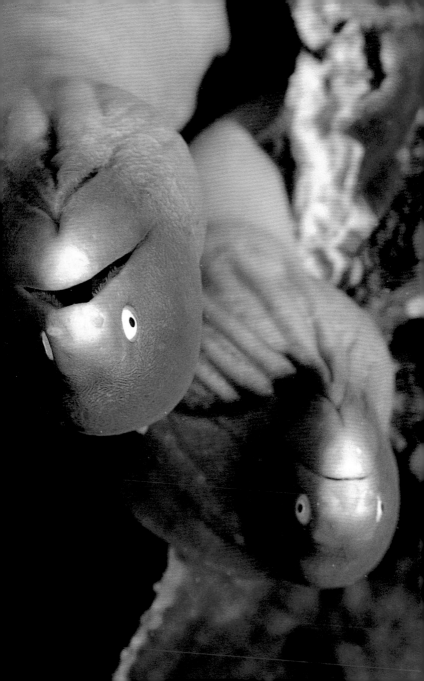

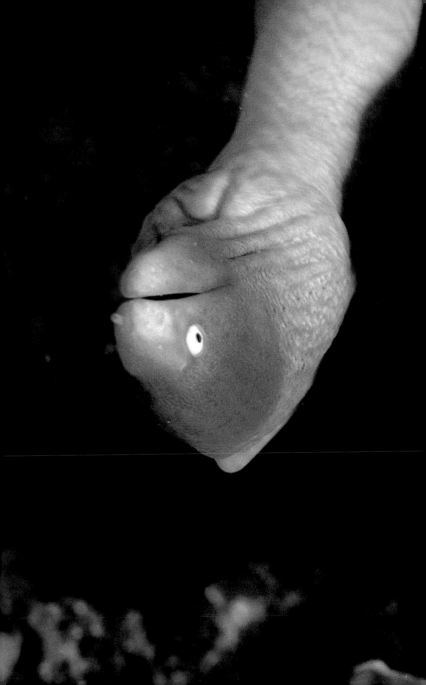

Harlequin tusk fish, Great Barrier Reef, Australia, 1999

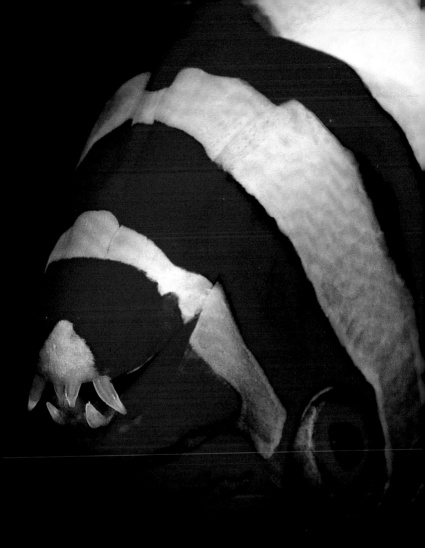

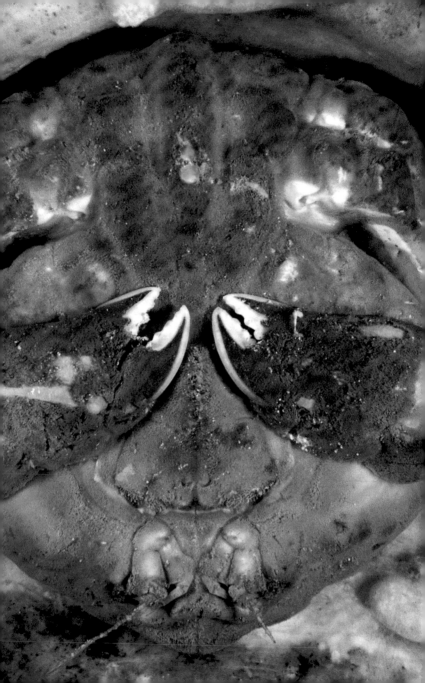

Sponge crab, Shark Bay, Western Australia, 1989
Overleaf: Tiger shark, Aliwal Shoals, South Africa, 2003

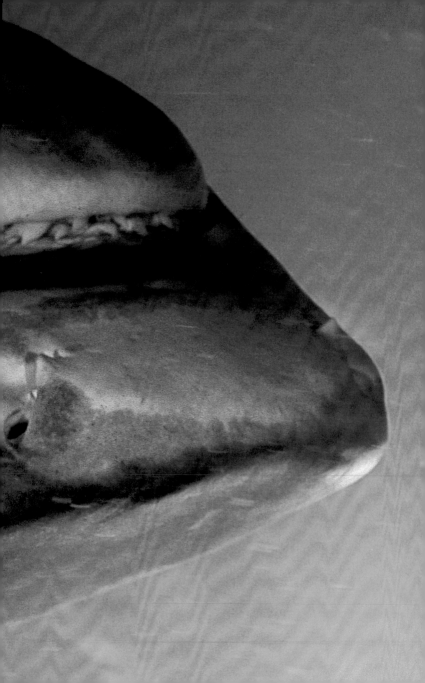

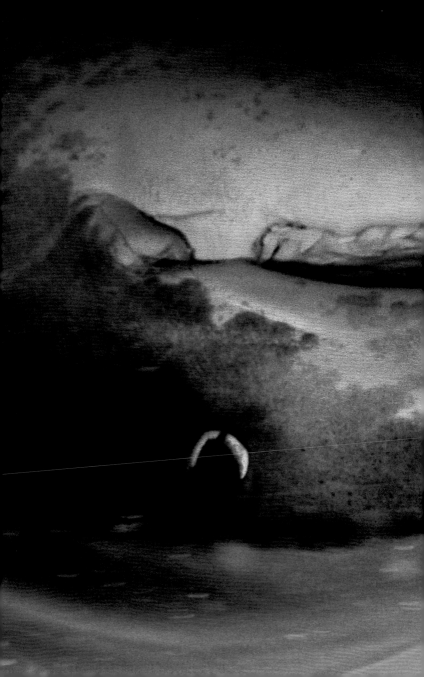

Marbled snake eel, Milne Bay, Papua New Guinea, 199

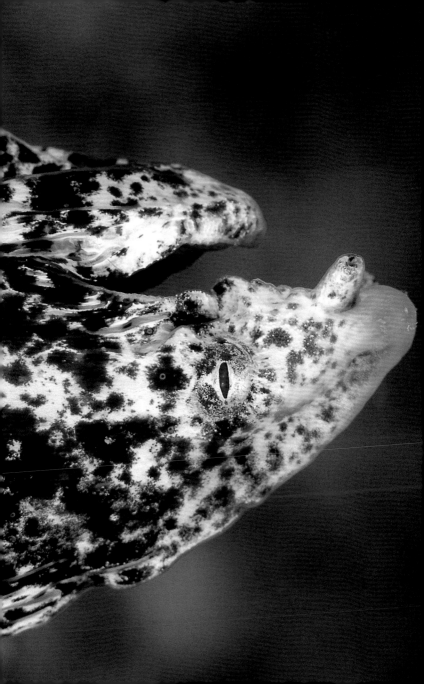

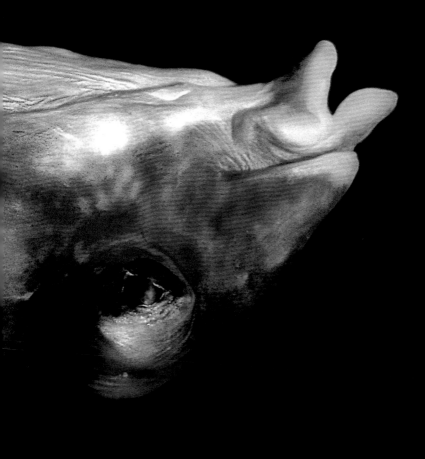

Sea robin, Tasmania, Australia, 1998
Overleaf: Snake eel, Milne Bay,
Papua New Guinea, 1986

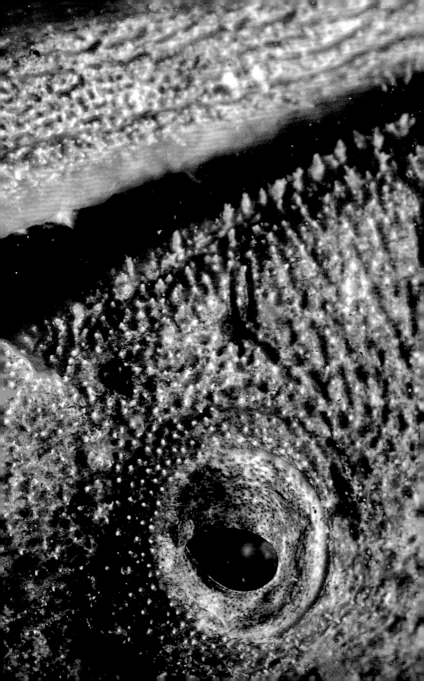

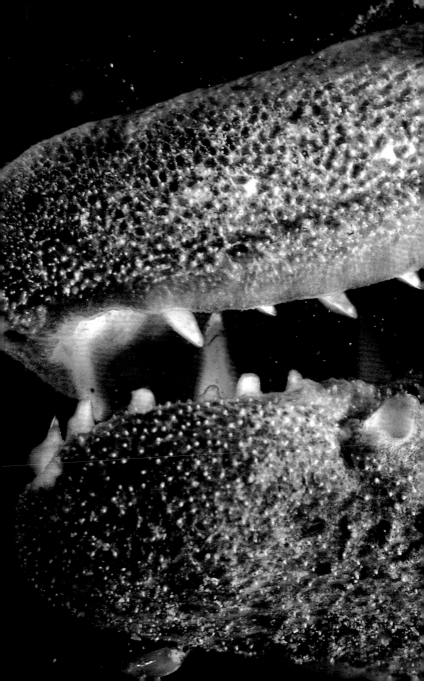

Potbellied sea horse, Tasmania, Australia, 1995

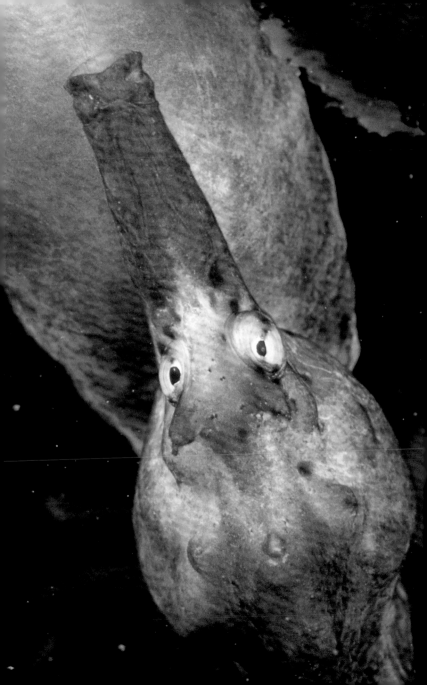

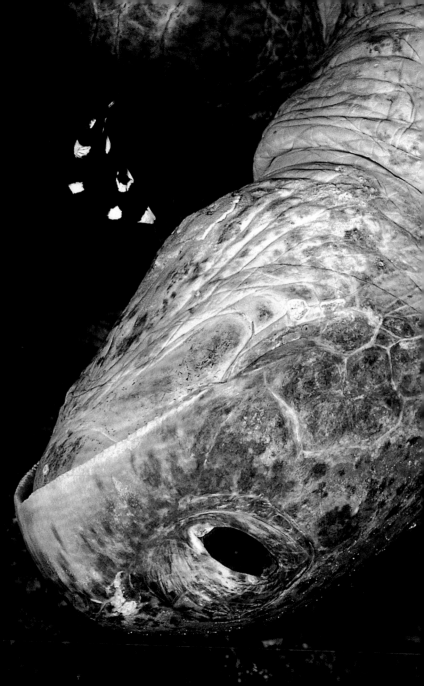

Green turtle and juvenile wrasse, Great Barrier Reef,
Australia, 1989
Overleaf: Long-nosed hawk fish, Bali, Indonesia, 1996

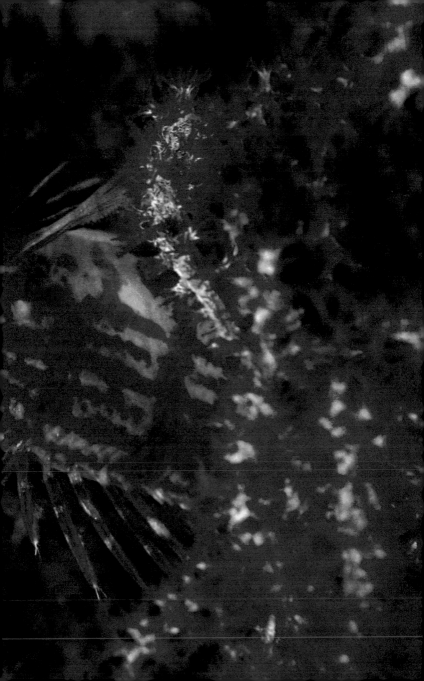

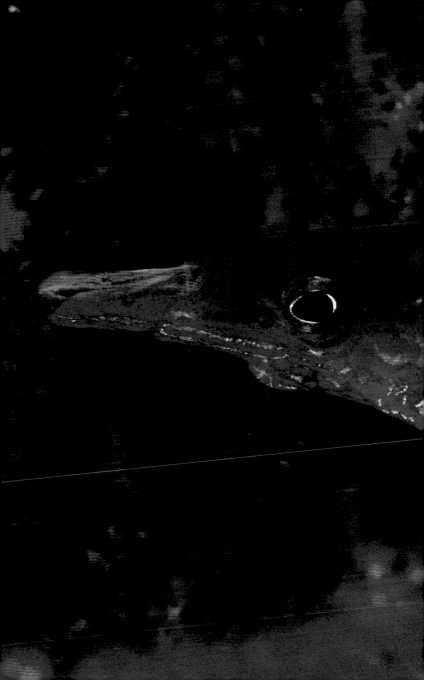

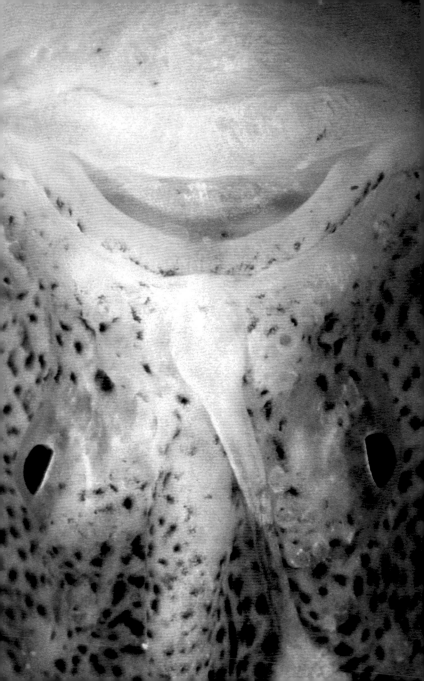

Ziebell's hand fish, Tasmania, Australia, 1995
Overleaf: Ziebell's hand fish, Tasmania, Australia, 1995

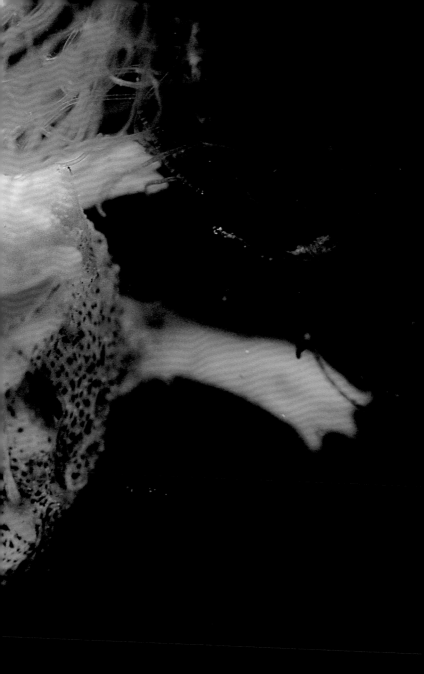

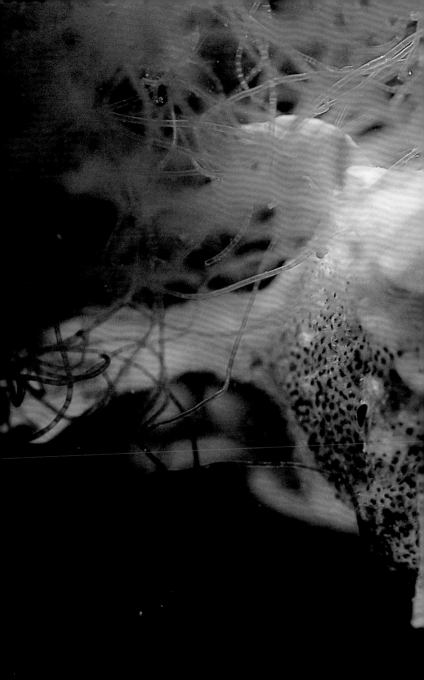

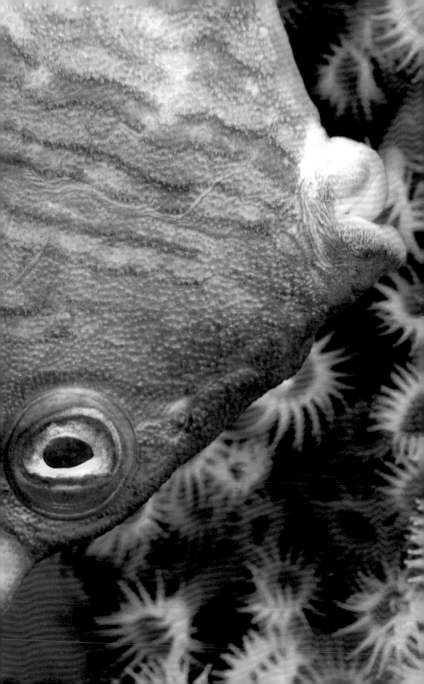

Cow fish, Tasmania, Australia, 1995
Overleaf: Sea moth (pegasus), Flores, Indonesia, 1996

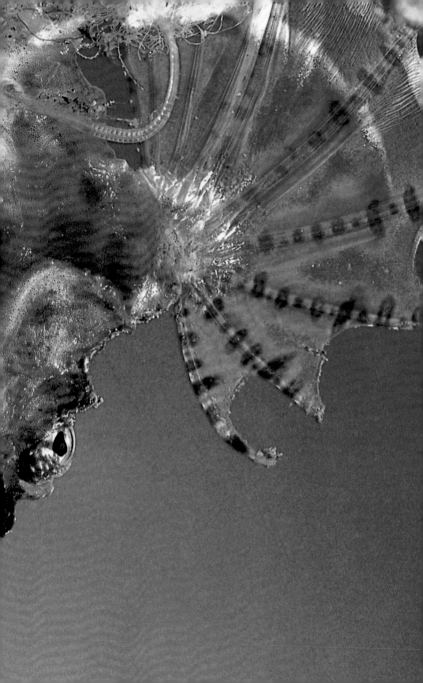

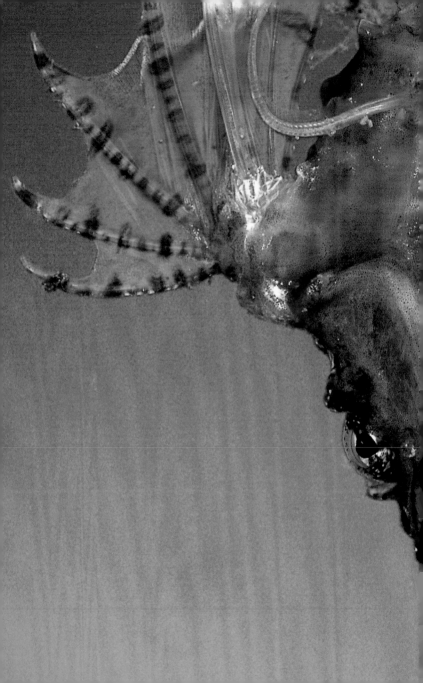

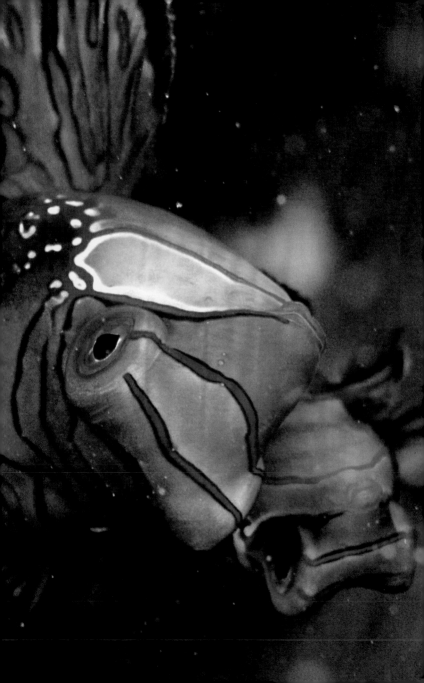

Mandarin fish, Koror, Palau, 1994
Overleaf: Weedy sea dragon, Tasmania, Australia, 1995

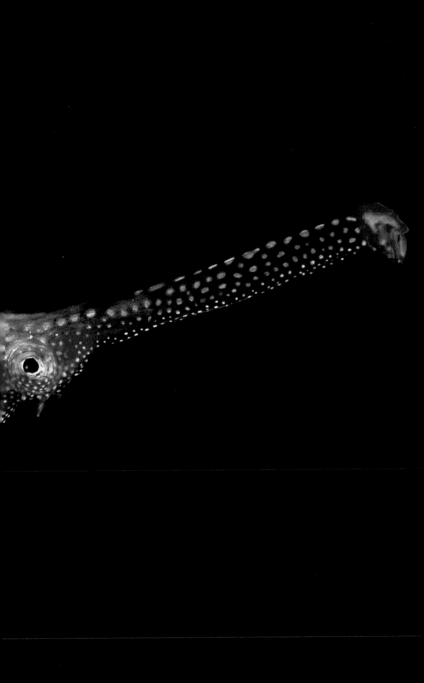

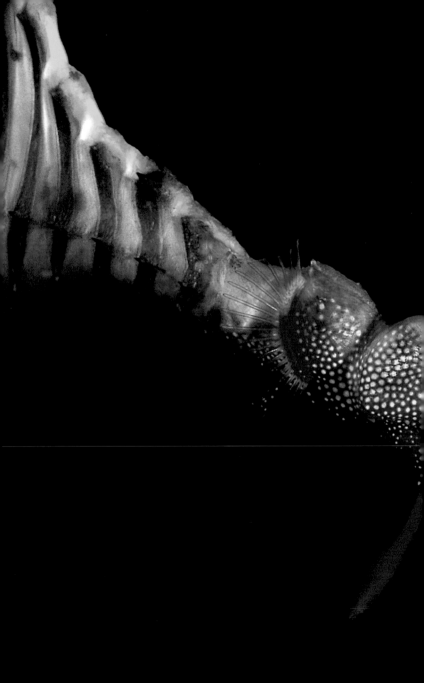

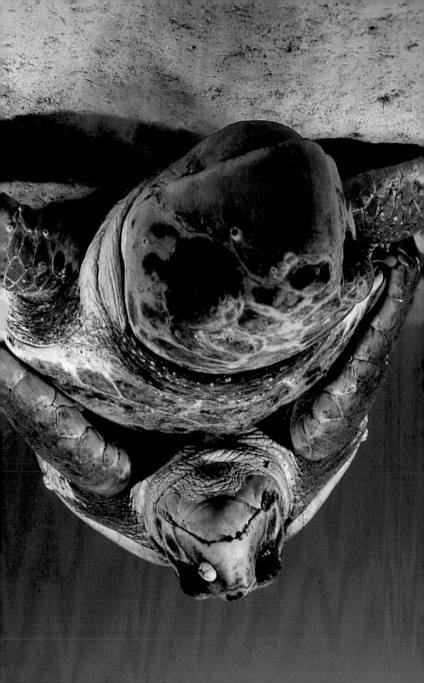

Mating Loggerhead turtles, Florida Keys, USA, 1998
Overleaf: Mating Loggerhead turtles, Florida Keys,
USA, 1998

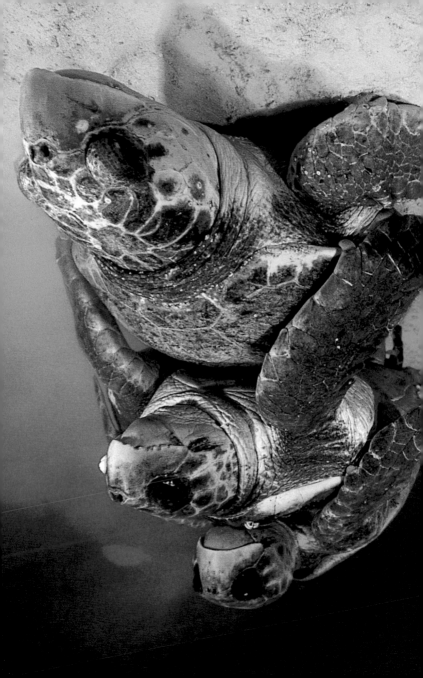

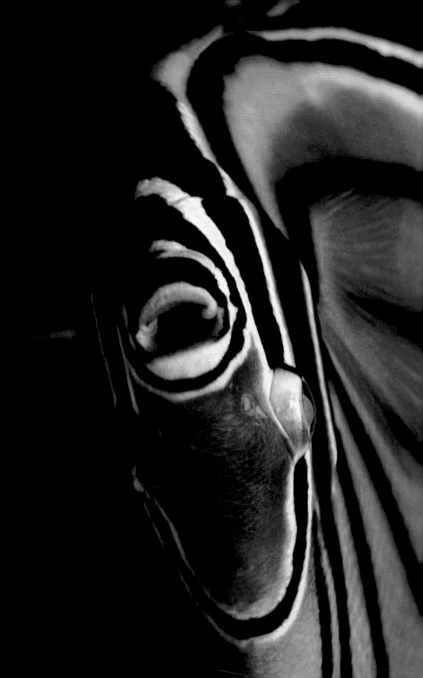

Meyer's butterfly fish, Kimbe Bay,
Papua New Guinea, 1986
Overleaf: Scorpion fish, Poor Knights Islands,
New Zealand, 1986

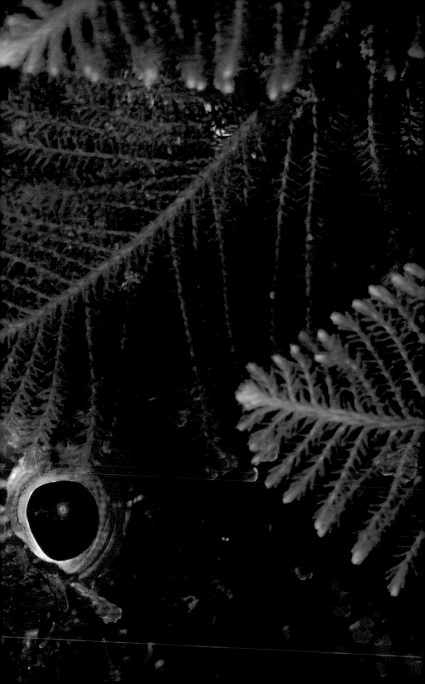

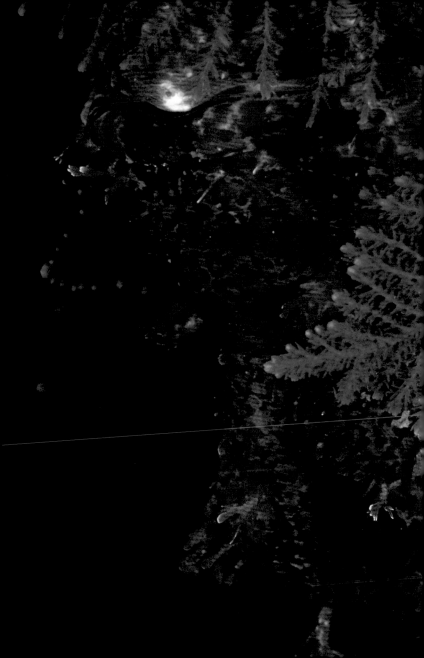

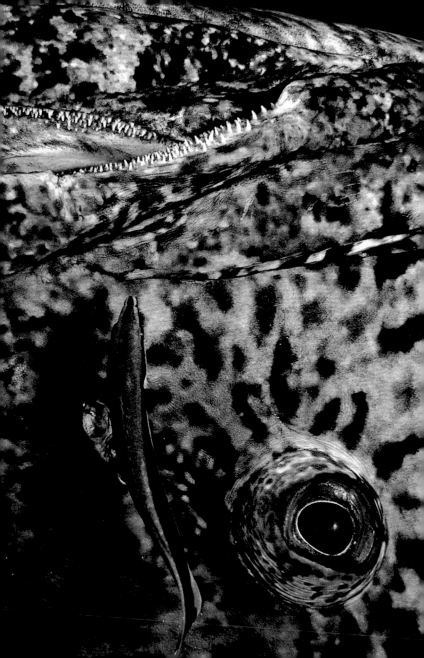

Potato cod and Cleaner wrasse, Great Barrier Reef,
Australia, 1989
Overleaf: Potato cod and Cleaner wrasse,
Great Barrier Reef, Australia, 1989

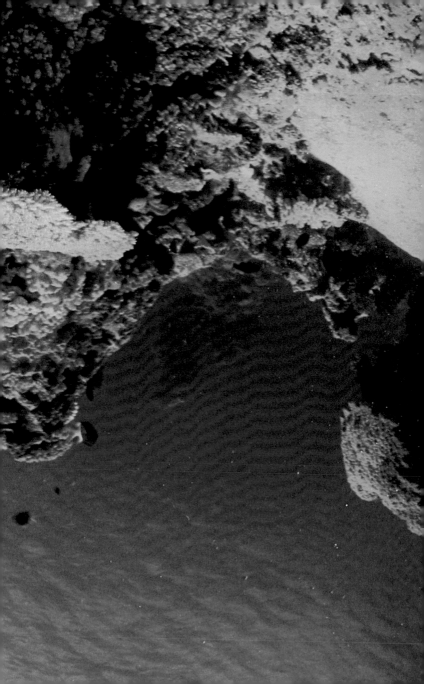

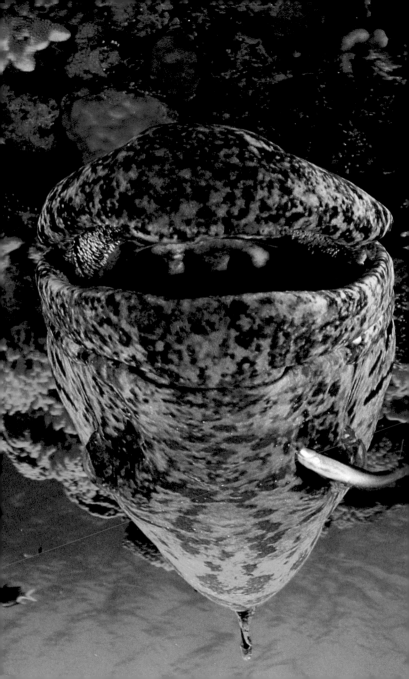

Hawk fish, Izu, Japan, 1982

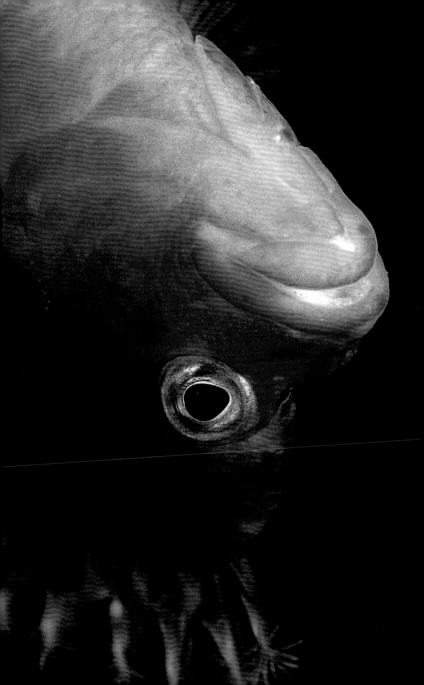

Reef cuttle fish, Great Barrier Reef, Australia, 1999

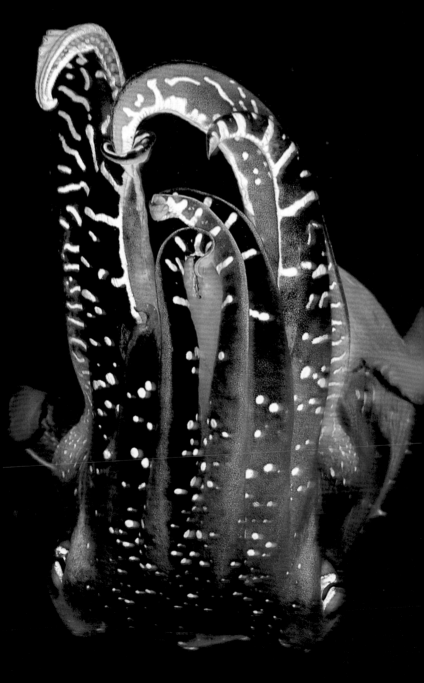

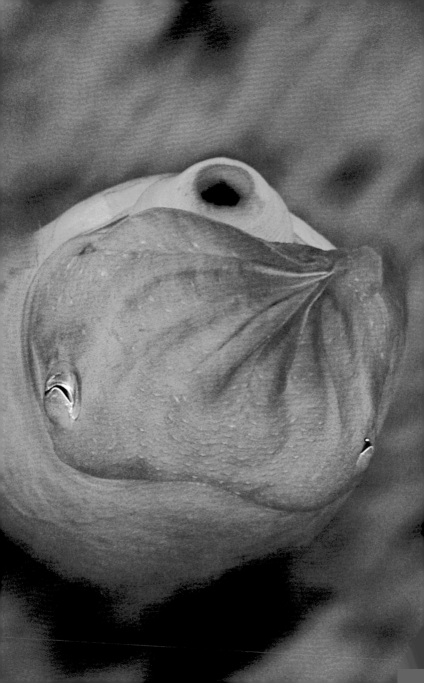

Reef cuttle fish, Great Barrier Reef, Australia, 1999
Overleaf: Rhinopias scorpion fish, Milne Bay,
Papua New Guinea, 1996

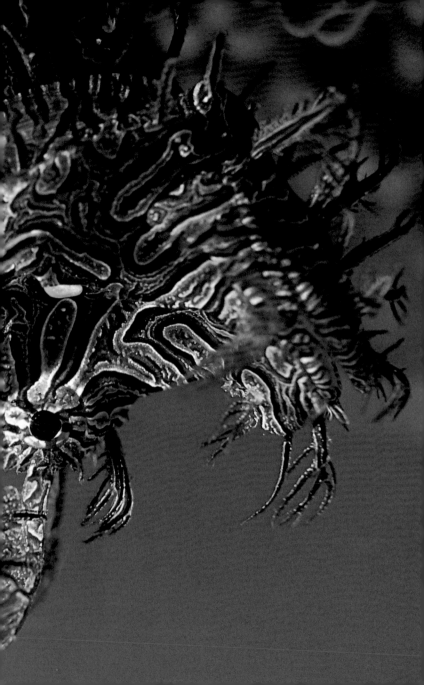

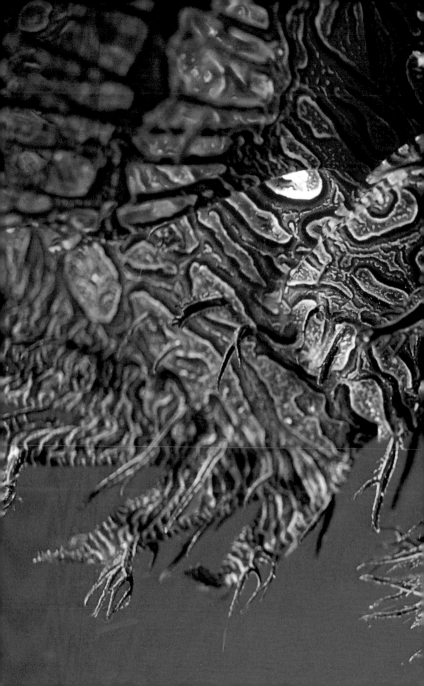

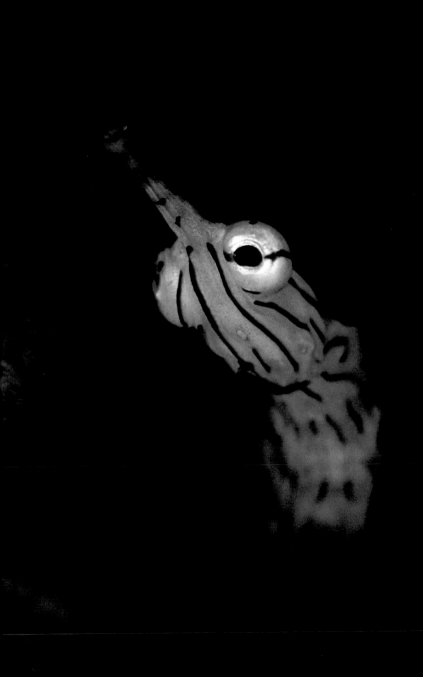

Pipe fish, Mabul, Malaysia, 1996
Overleaf: Angler fish, Izu, Japan, 1981

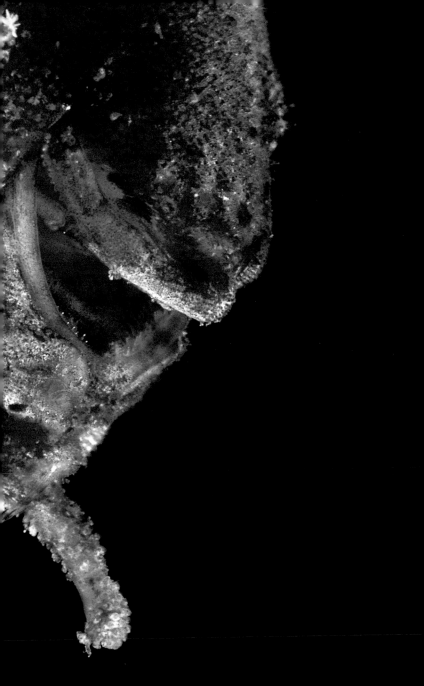

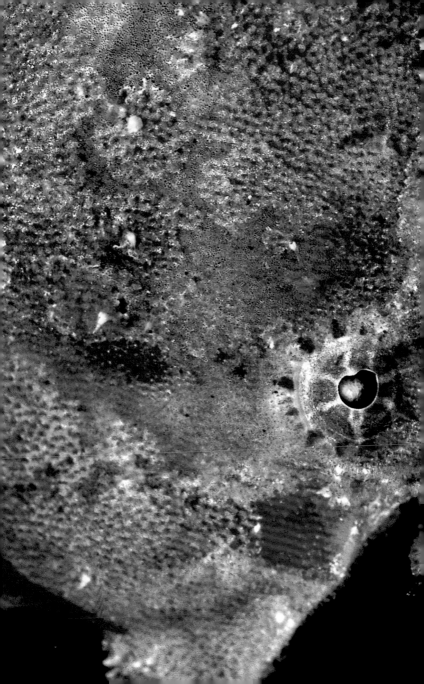

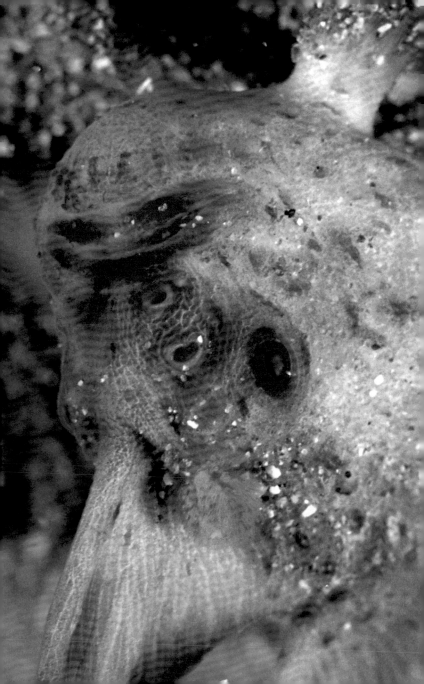

Red hand fish, Tasmania, Australia, 1995
Overleaf: A pair of Red hand fish, Tasmania,
Australia, 1995

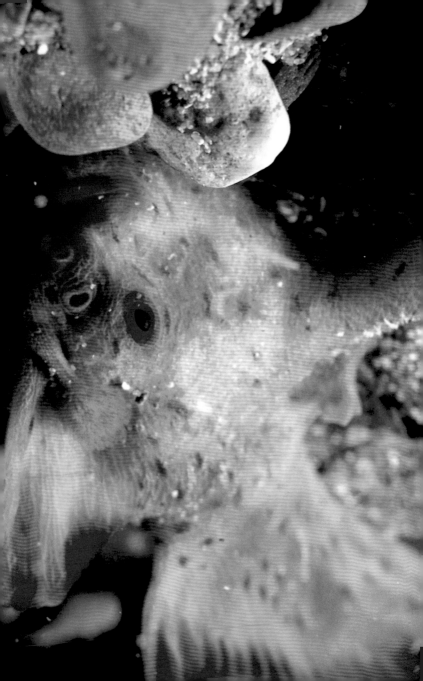

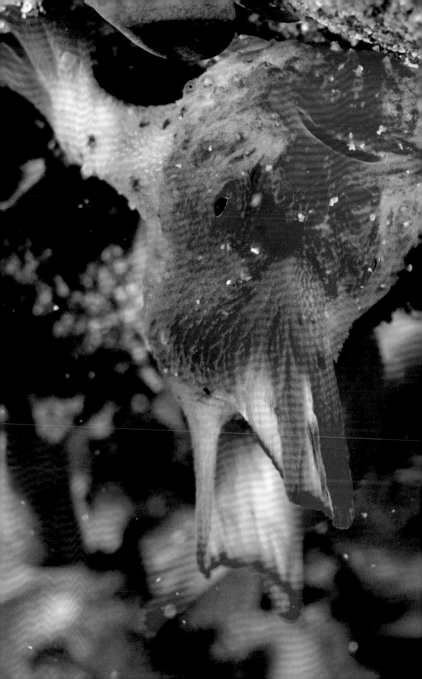

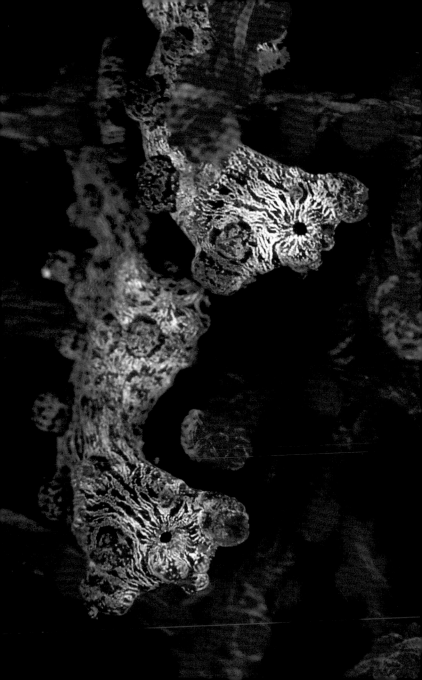

Pygmy sea horses, Kungkungan Bay, Indonesia, 2001
Overleaf: Stargazer, Kungkungan Bay, Indonesia, 2001

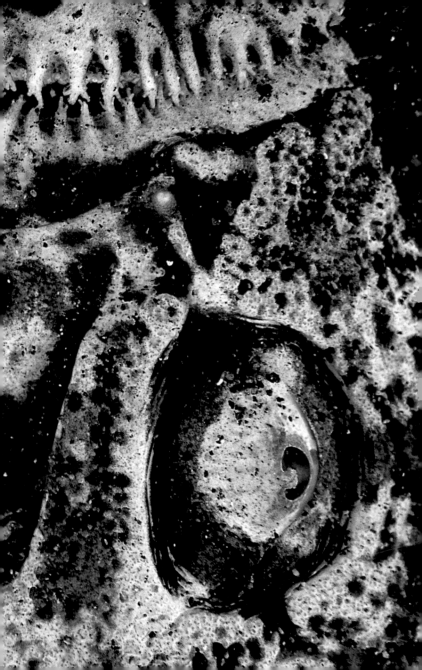

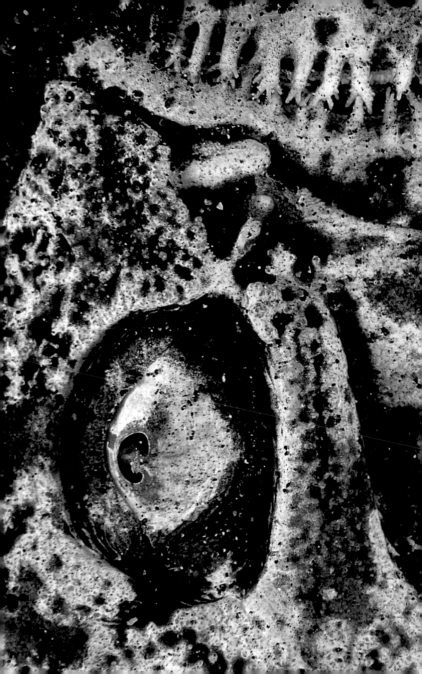

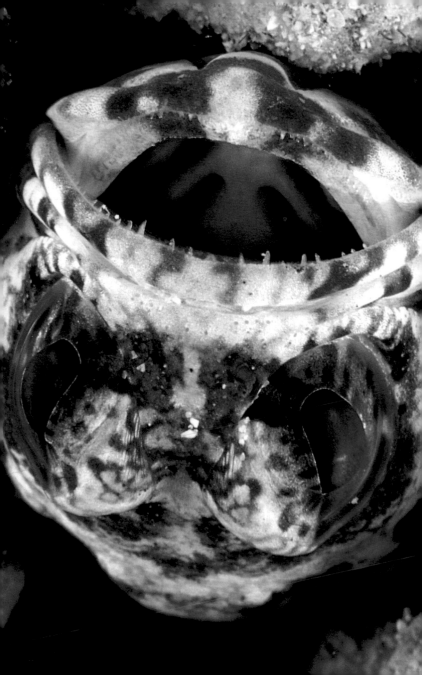

Jaw fish, Cayo Largo, Cuba, 2000
Overleaf: Bandtooth conger eel, Isle of Youth,
Cuba, 2000

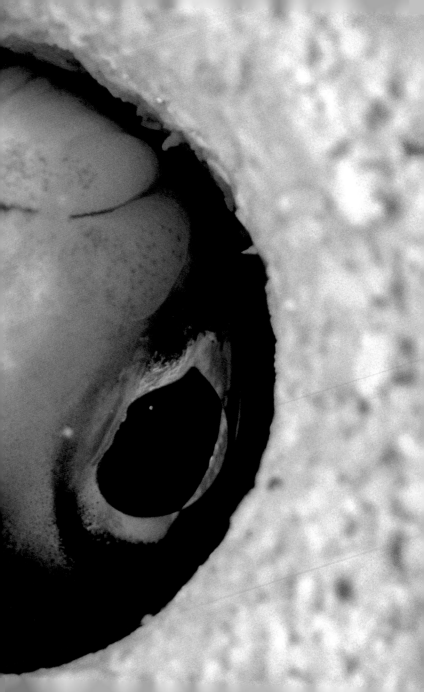

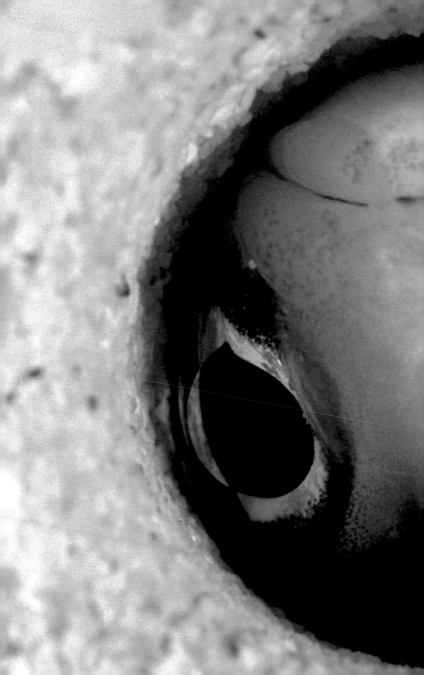

Cow fish, Tasmania, Australia, 1995

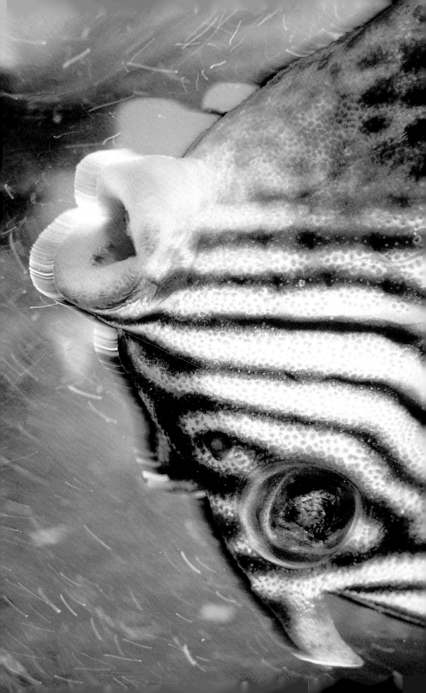

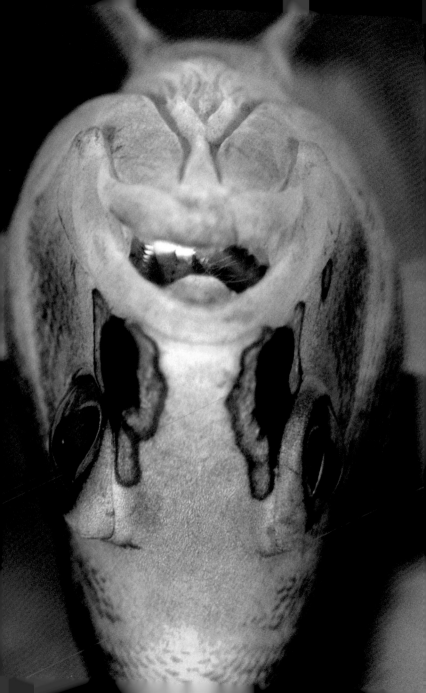

Yellow hamlet, Cayo Largo, Cuba, 2000
Overleaf: Giant cuttle fish, Tasmania, Australia, 1995

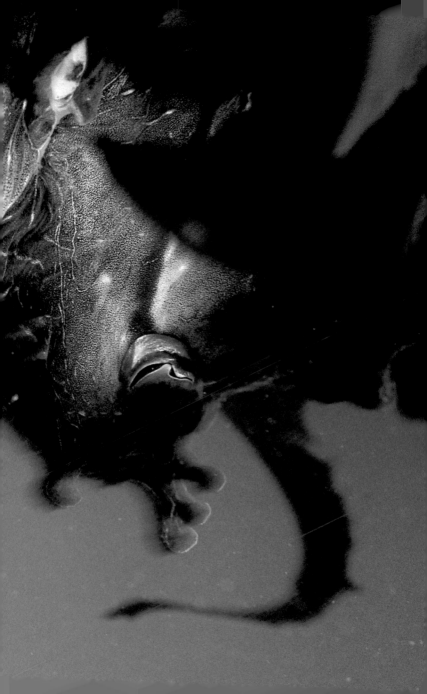

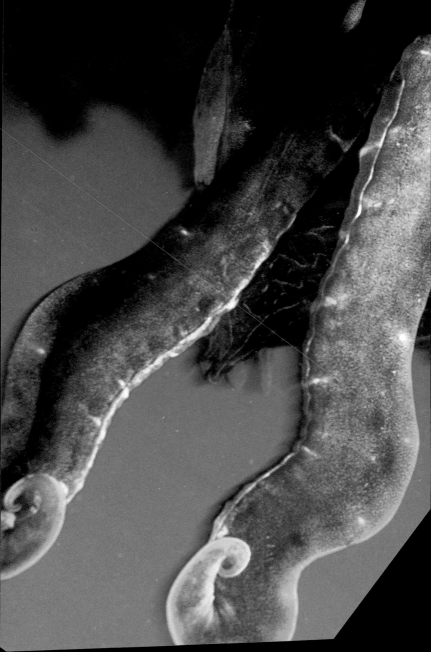

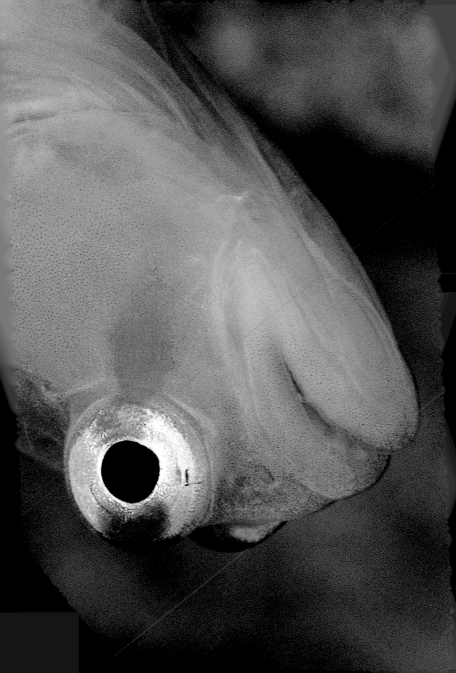

Randall's shrimp goby, Bali, Indonesia, 1996
Overleaf: Spotted hawk fish, Galapagos Islands,
Ecuador, 1998

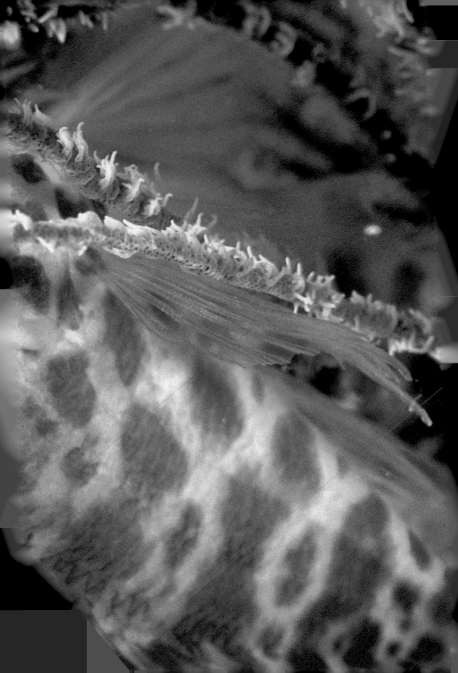

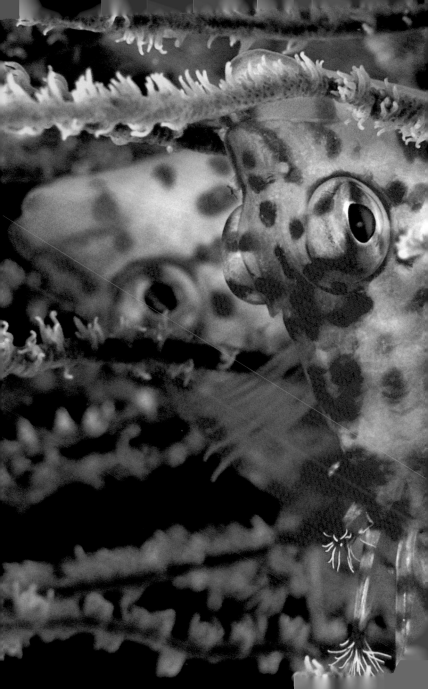

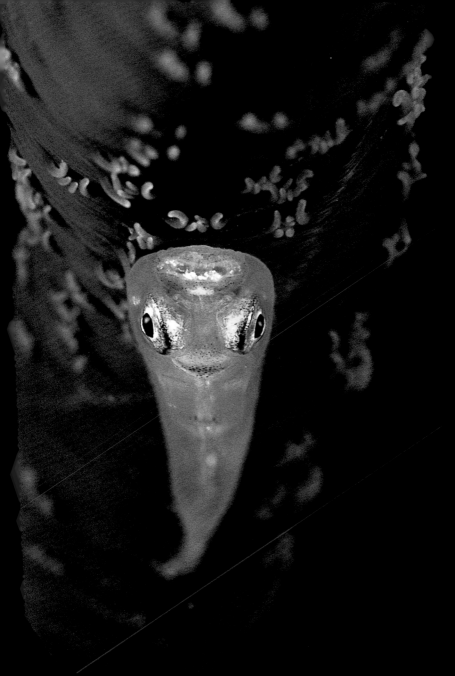

Whip coral goby, Great Barrier Reef, Australia, 1999
Overleaf: Leafy sea dragon, Adelaide,
South Australia, 1984

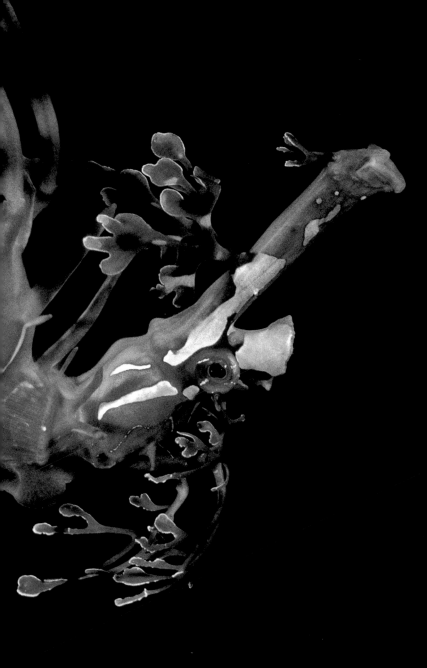

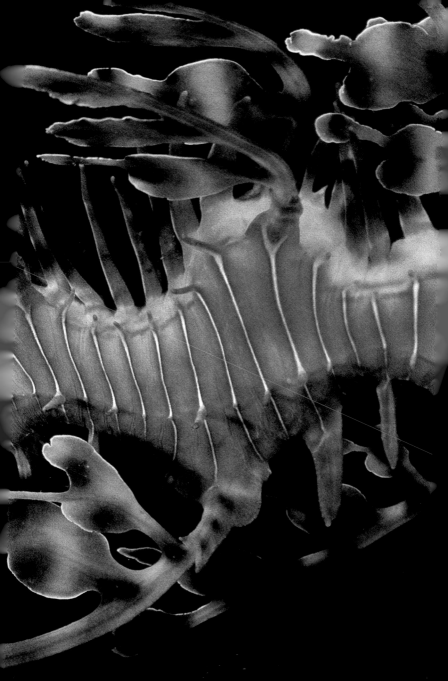

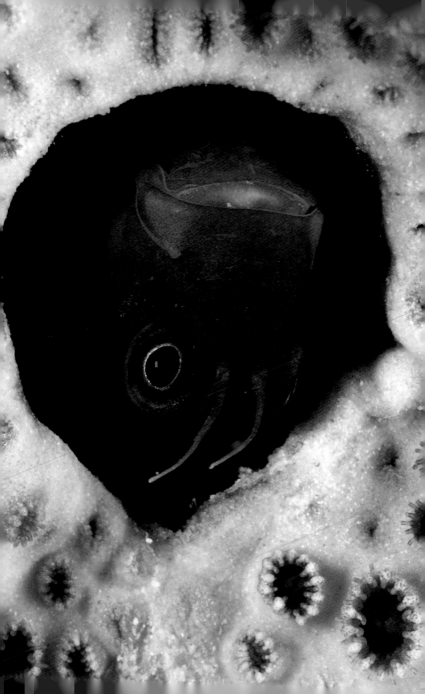

Bicolour blenny, Great Barrier Reef, Australia, 1989
Overleaf: Weed fish, Ewens Ponds,
South Australia, 1981

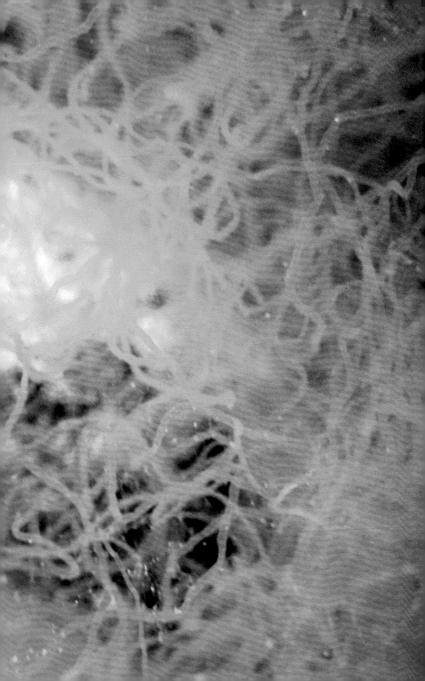

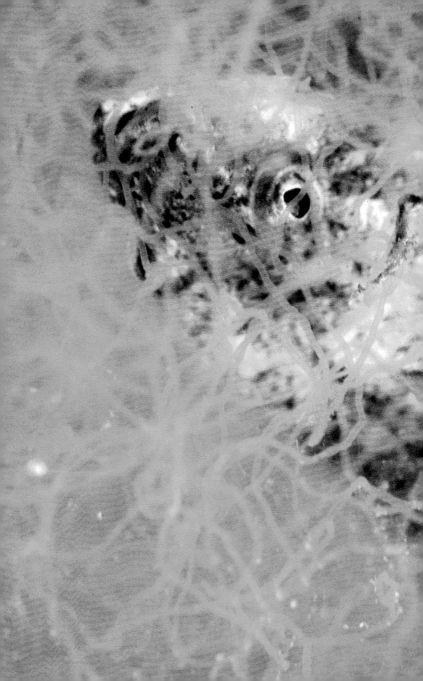

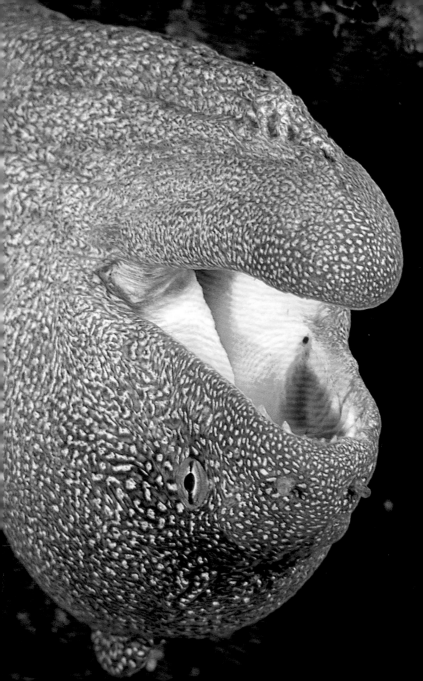

Yellowmouth moray eel, Aliwal Shoals,
South Africa, 2002
Overleaf: Rhinopias scorpion fish, Milne Bay,
Papua New Guinea, 1996

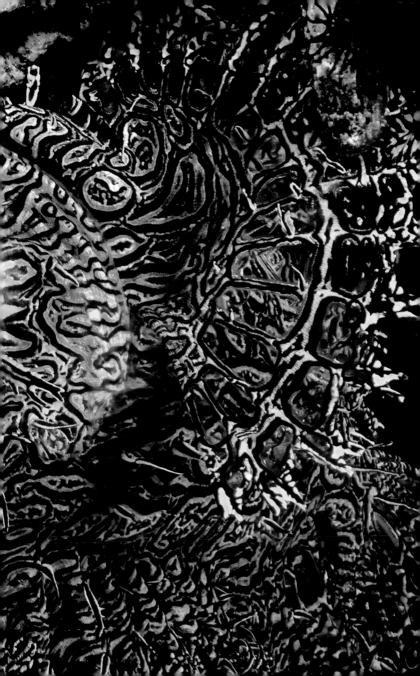

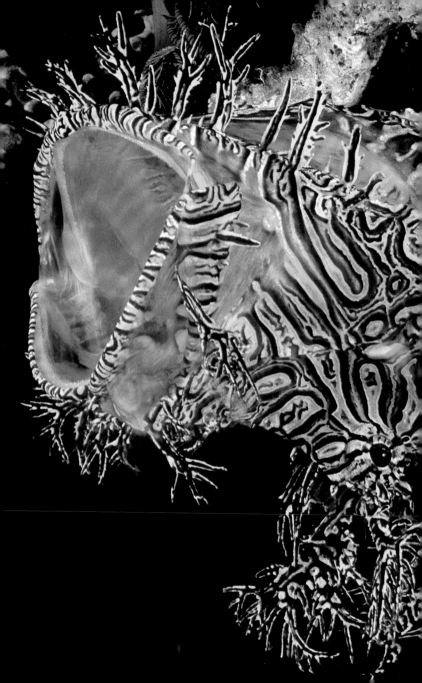

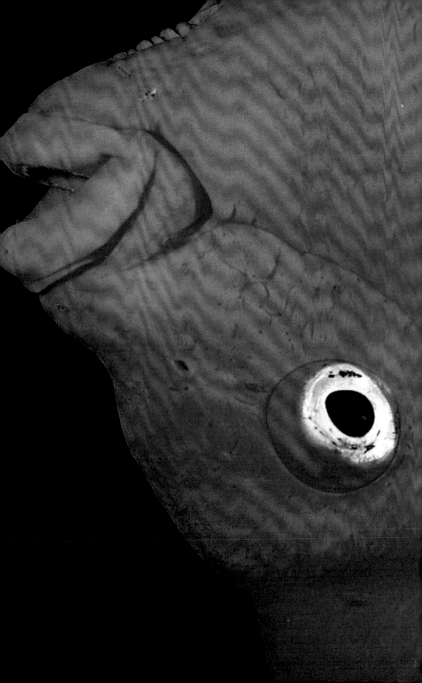

Garibaldi fish, Channel Islands, California, USA, 1997
Overleaf: Flowery flounder, Kungkungan Bay,
Indonesia, 2001

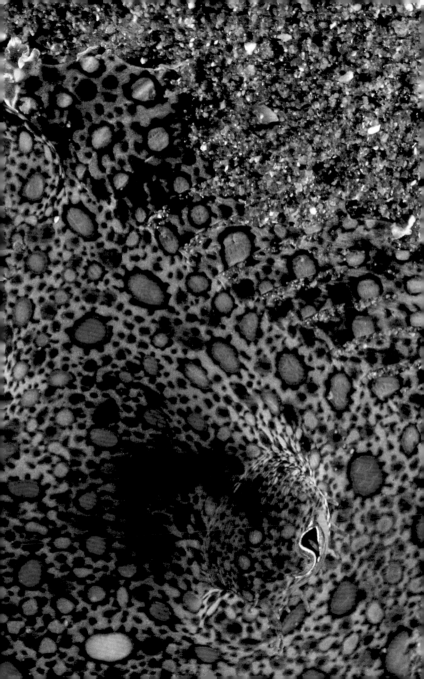

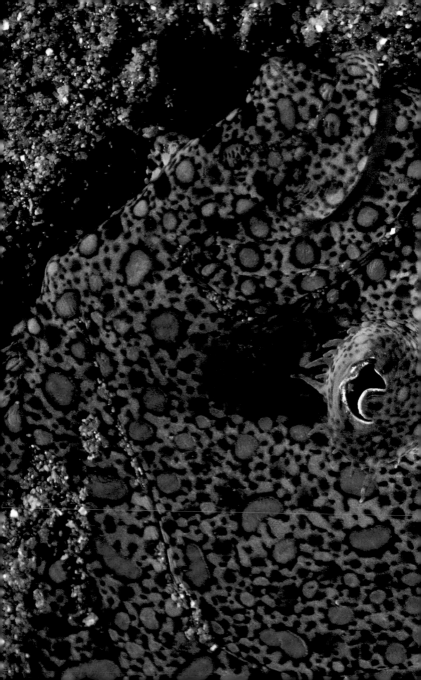

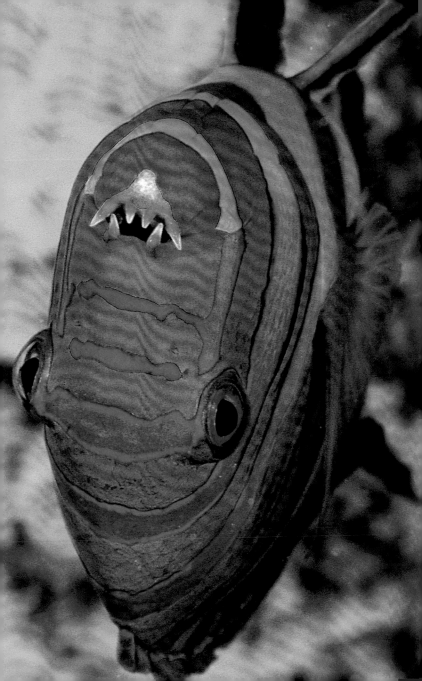

Harlequin tusk fish, Great Barrier Reef, Australia, 1999
Overleaf: Reef squid, Isle of Youth, Cuba, 2000

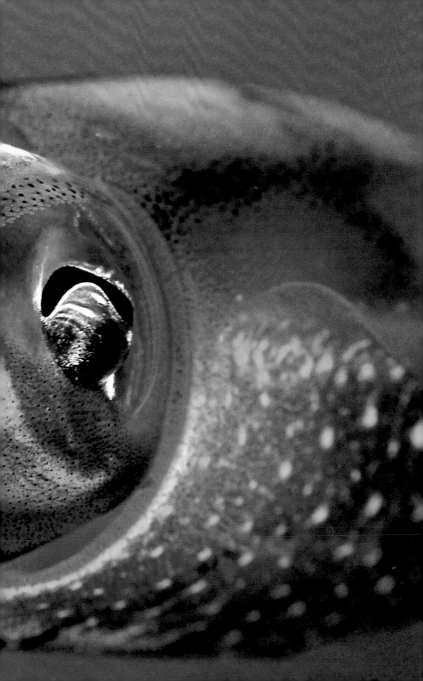

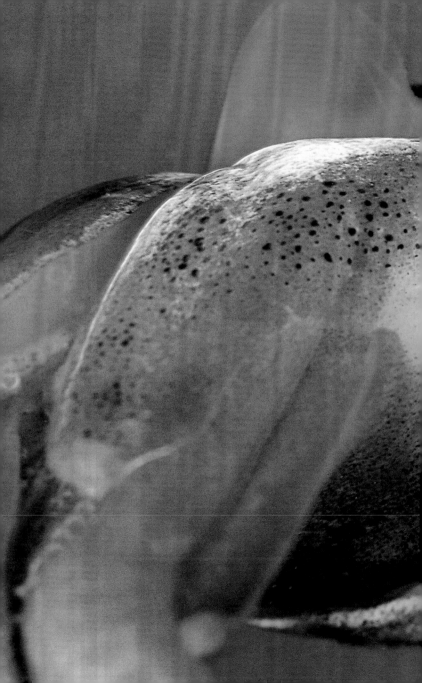

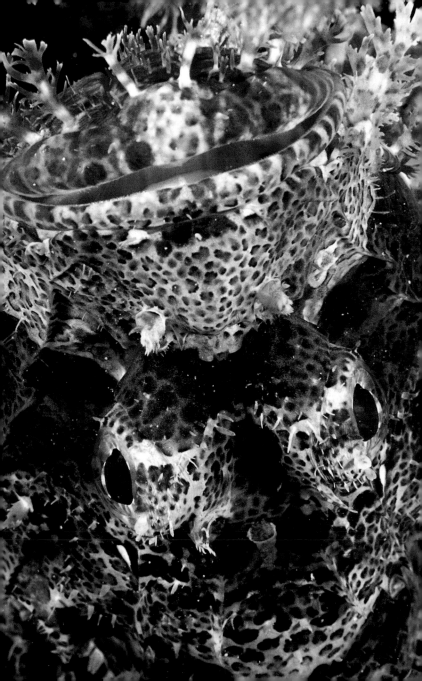

Monkey-faced scorpion fish, Flores, Indonesia, 1996
Overleaf: Stone fish, Great Barrier Reef, Australia, 1999

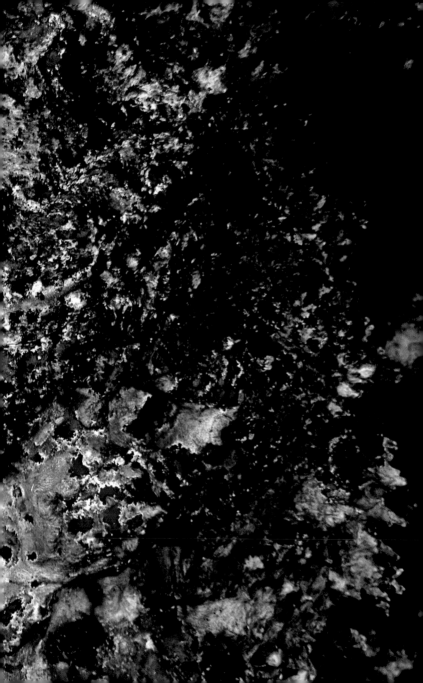

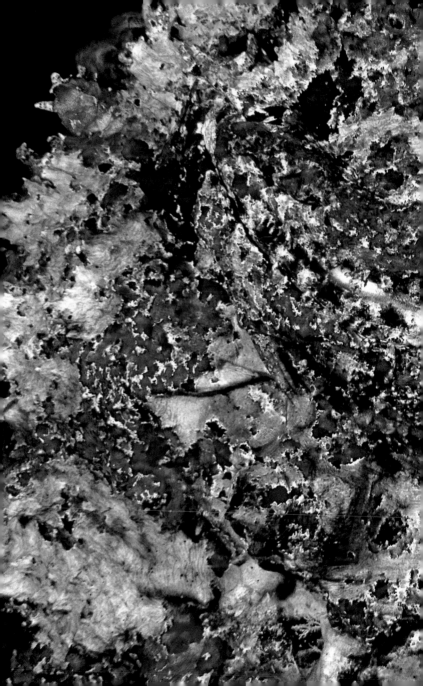

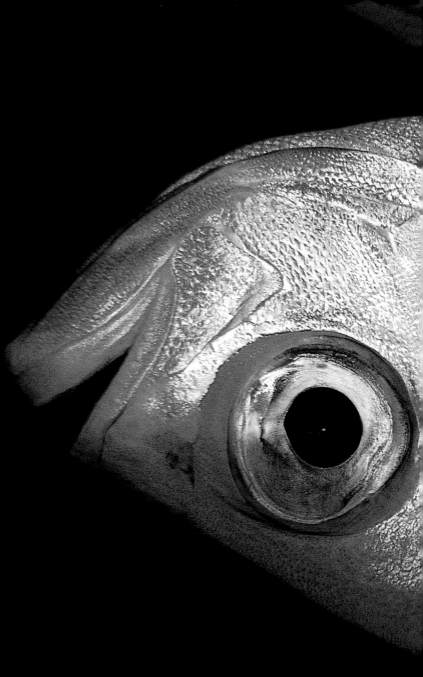

Glass-eye snapper, Grand Cayman Island, 1984
Overleaf: Sea horse, Izu, Japan, 1982

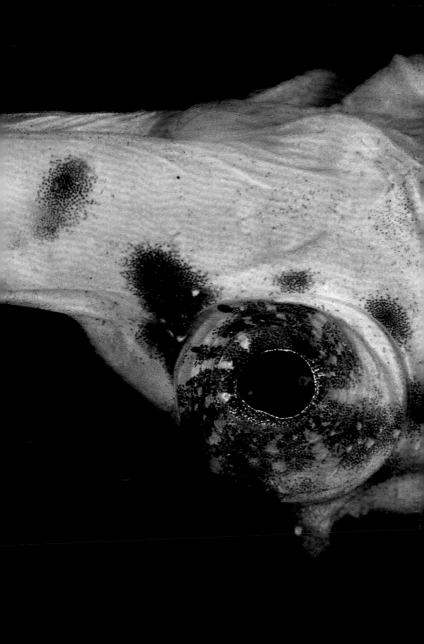

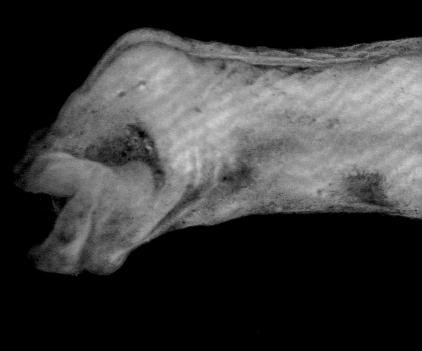

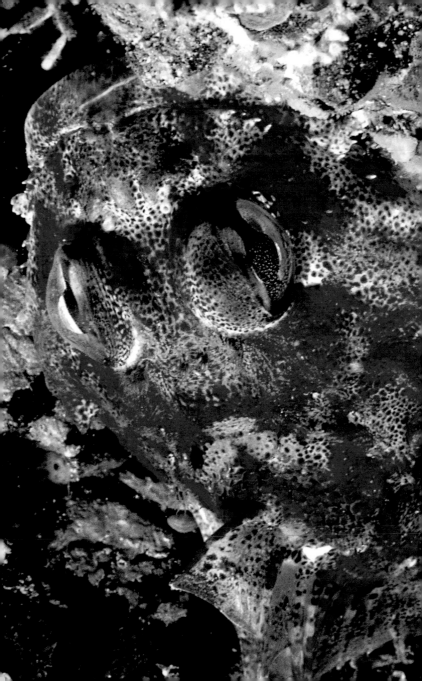

Red Irish lord, Vancouver Island, Canada, 1980
Overleaf: Tongue sole, Kungkungan Bay,
Indonesia, 2001

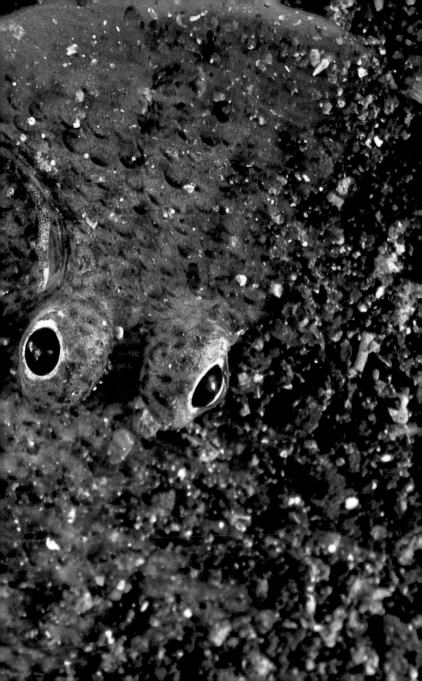

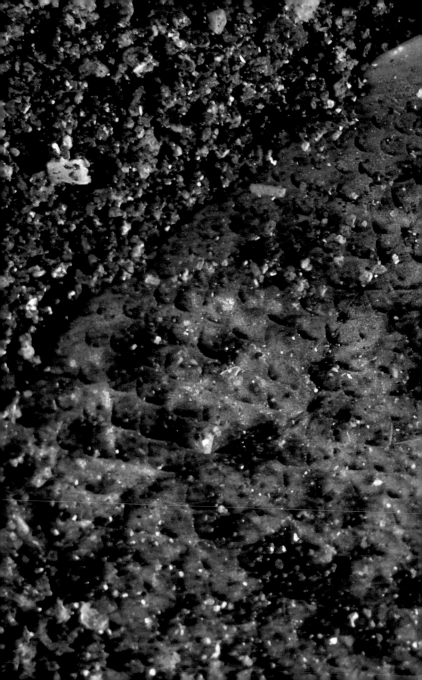

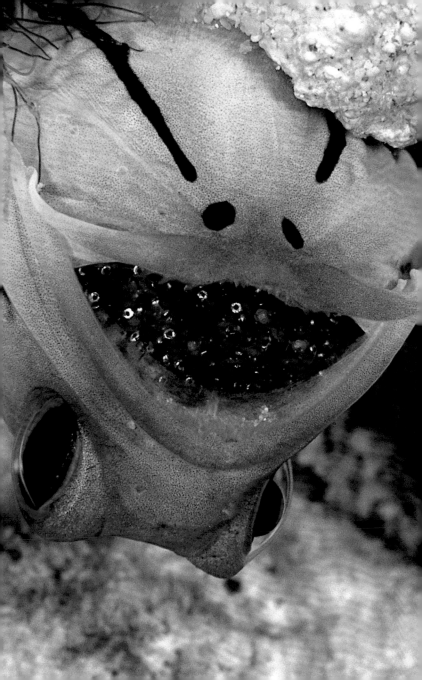

Yellow-headed jaw fish with eggs, Cayo Largo,
Cuba, 2000
Overleaf: Red velvet fish, Tasmania, Australia, 1995

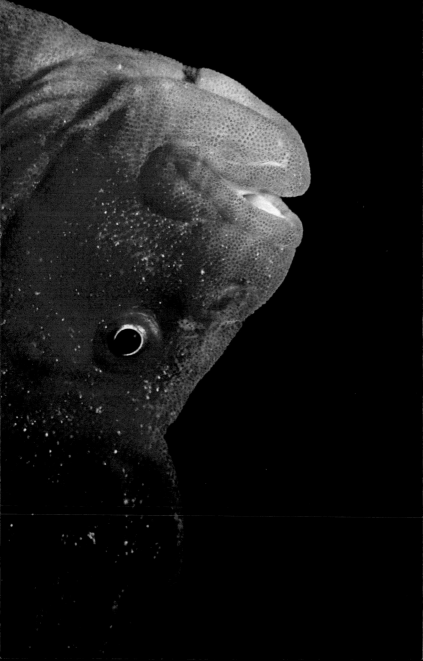

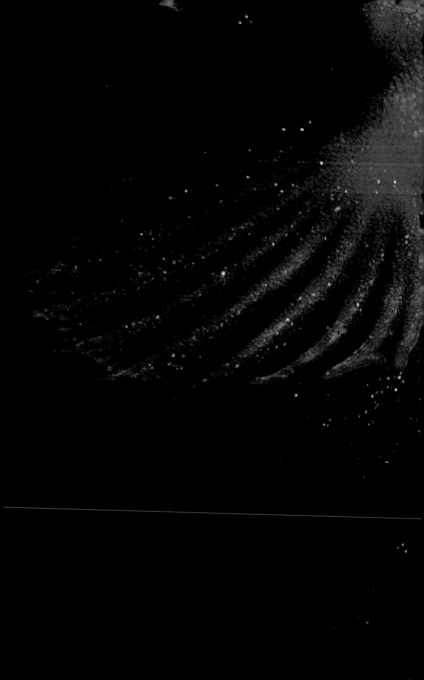

Semicircle angel fish, Kimbe Ba[y]
Papua New Guinea, 1995

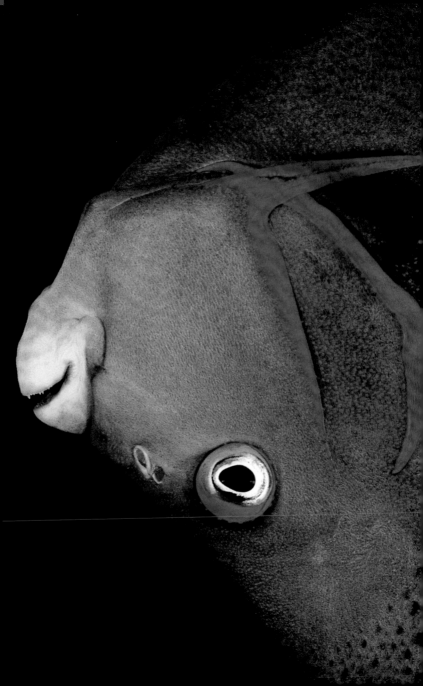

Soft coral goby, Bali, Indonesia, 1996

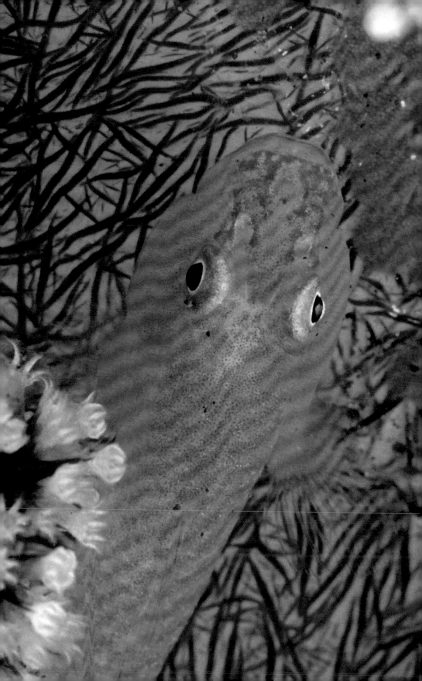

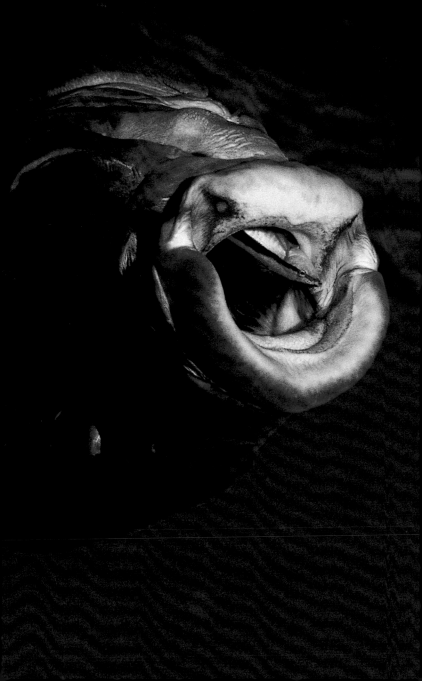

Sweetlips and Cleaner wrasse, Astove Atoll,
Seychelles, 1993
Overleaf: Blue-striped grunts, Florida Keys, USA, 1997

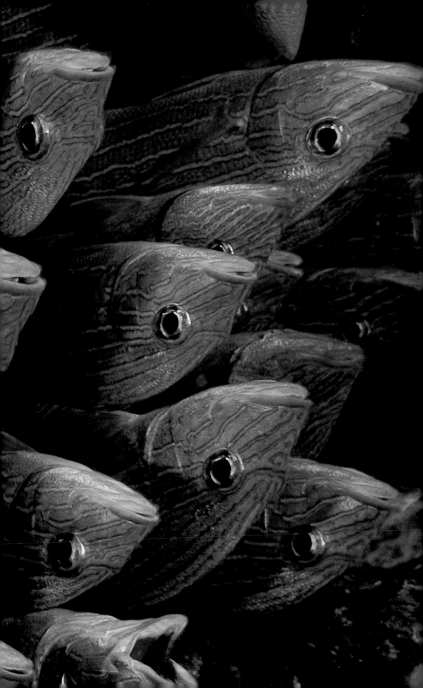

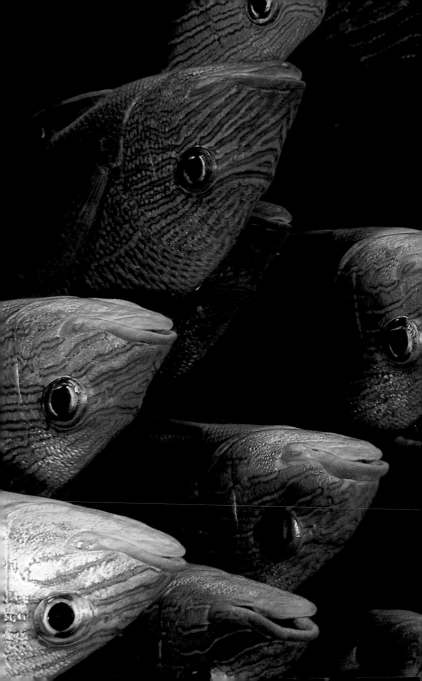

Barramundi cod, Great Barrier Reef, Australia, 1999

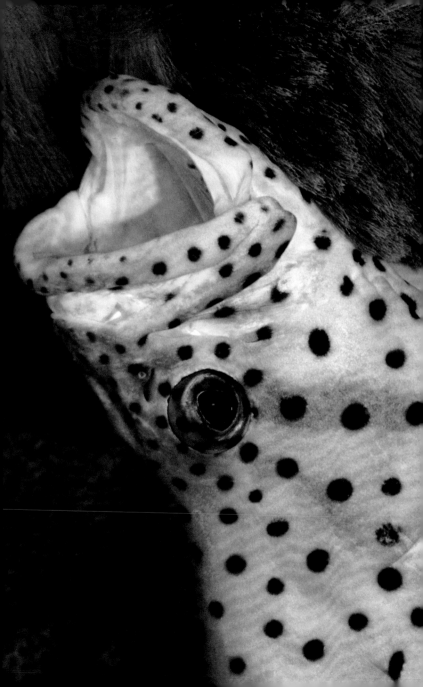

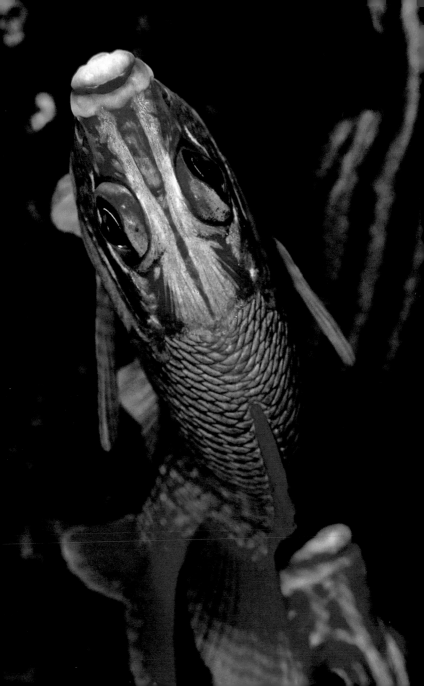

Giant squirrel fish, Peleliu Island, Palau, 2003
Overleaf: Porcupine fish, Grand Cayman Island, 1984

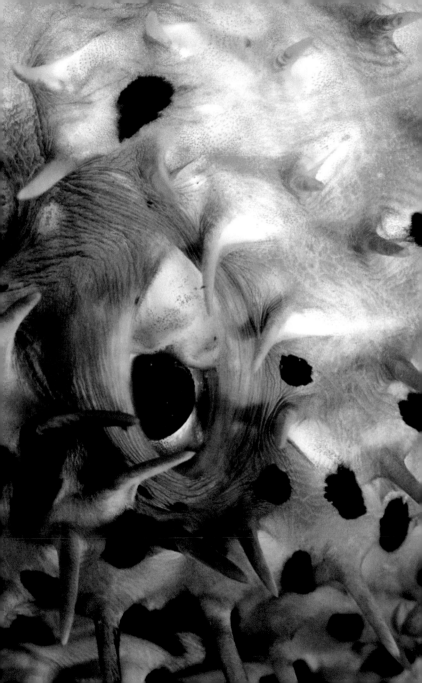

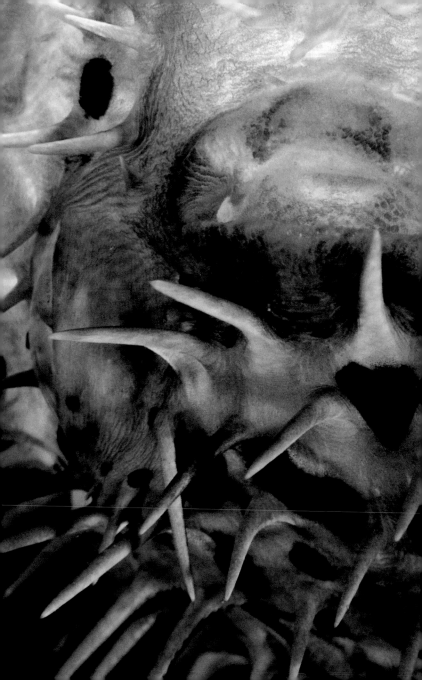

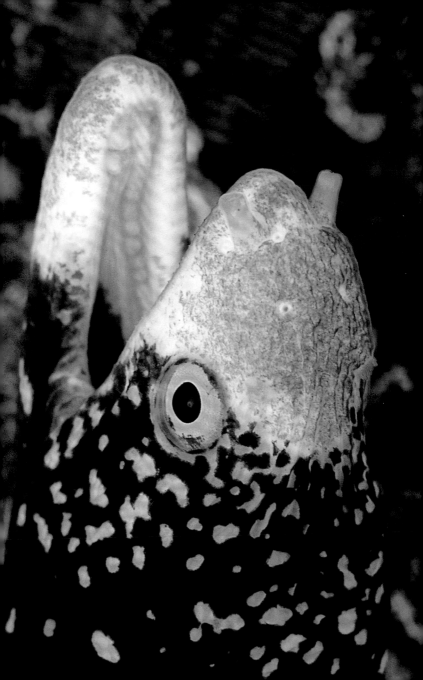

Snowflake moray eel, Great Barrier Reef,
Australia, 2000
Overleaf: Elephant fish, Tasmania, Australia, 1995

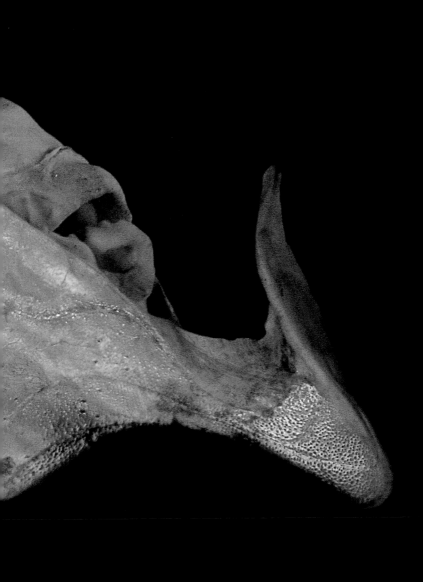

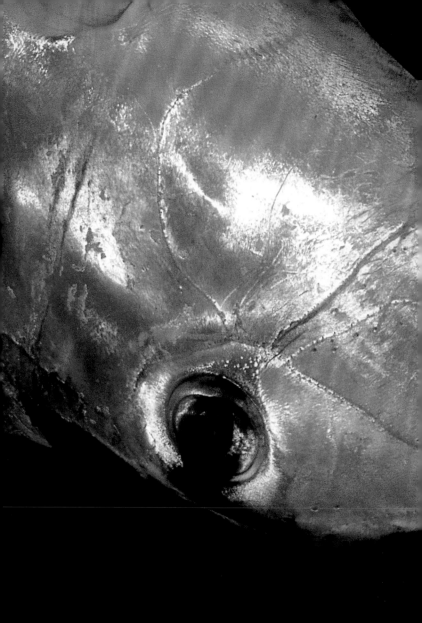

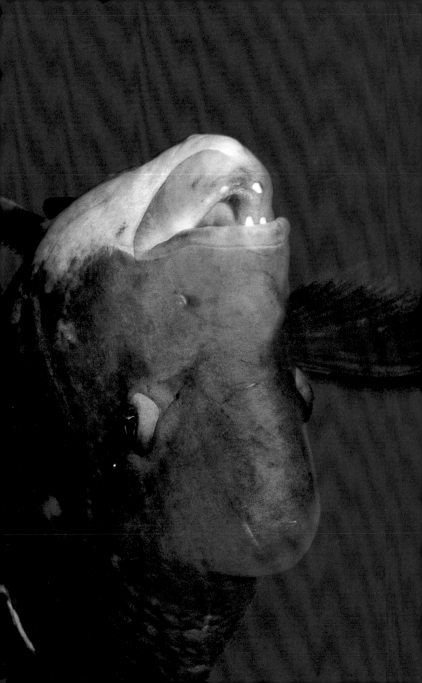

Steamer wrasse, Galapagos Islands, Ecuador, 1998
Overleaf: Toad fish, Exmouth, Western Australia, 2002

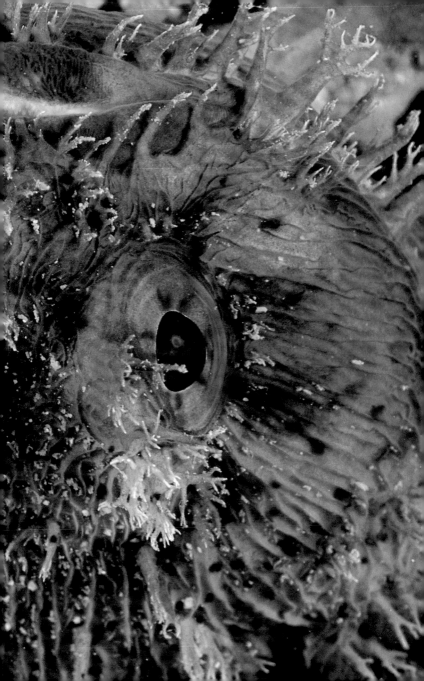

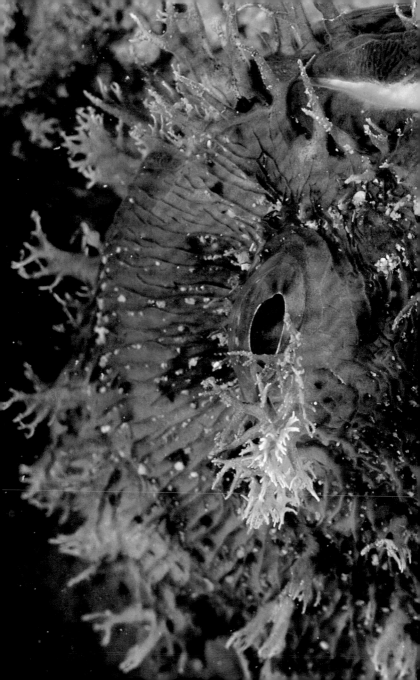

Flowery cod, Great Barrier Reef, Australia, 1999

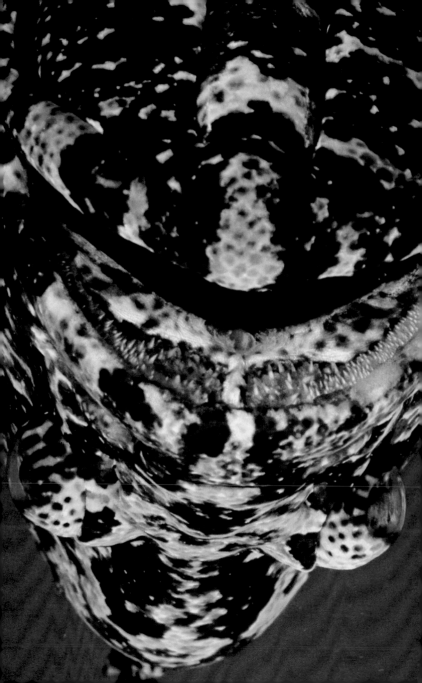

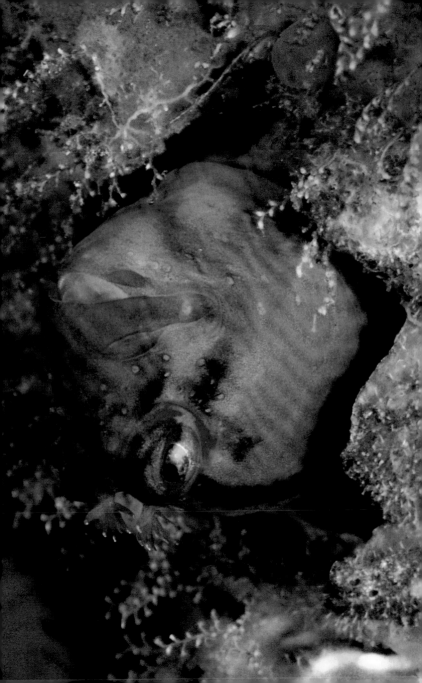

Blenny, Poor Knights Islands, New Zealand, 1986
Overleaf: Flashlight fish, Eilat, Israel, 1977

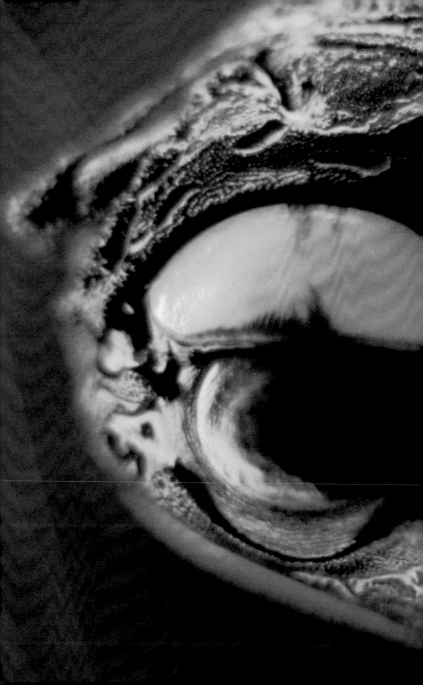

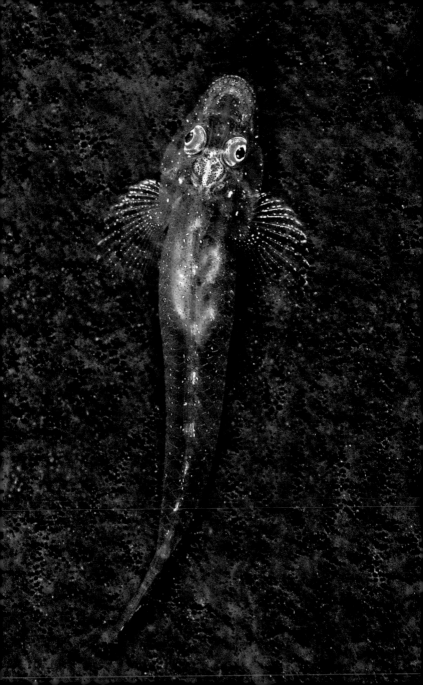

Goby on Elephant ear sponge, Bali, Indonesia, 1996
Overleaf: Stinging cat fish, Lord Howe Island,
Australia, 1986

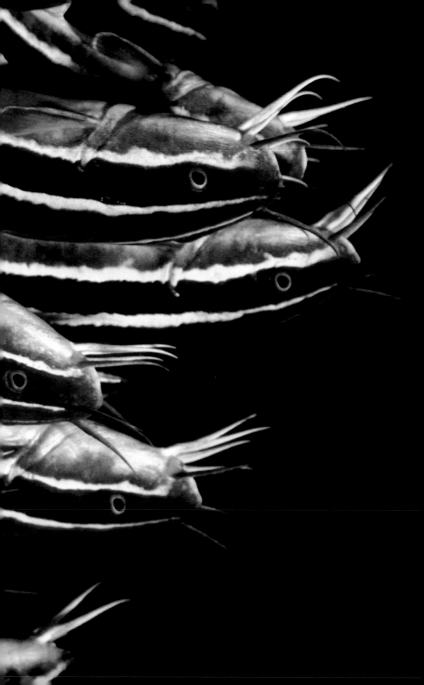

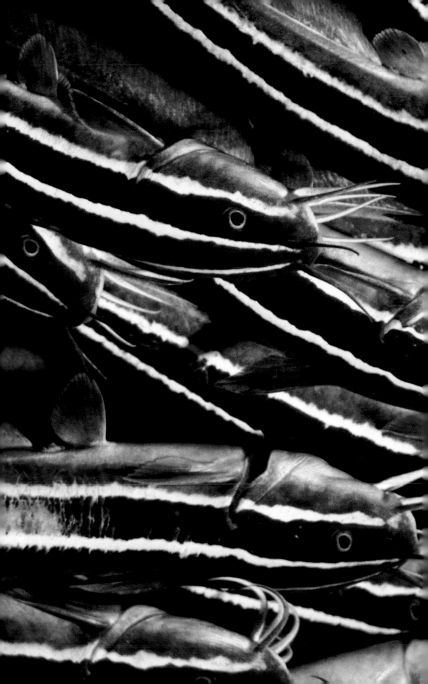

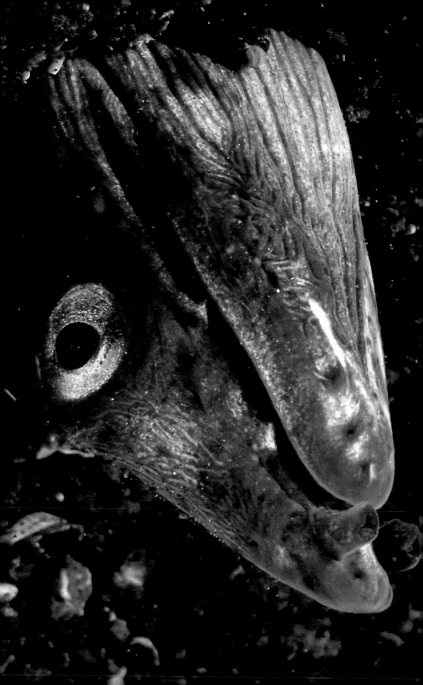

Snake eel, Kungkungan Bay, Indonesia, 2001
Overleaf: Spiny porcupine fish, Suruga Bay, Japan, 1989

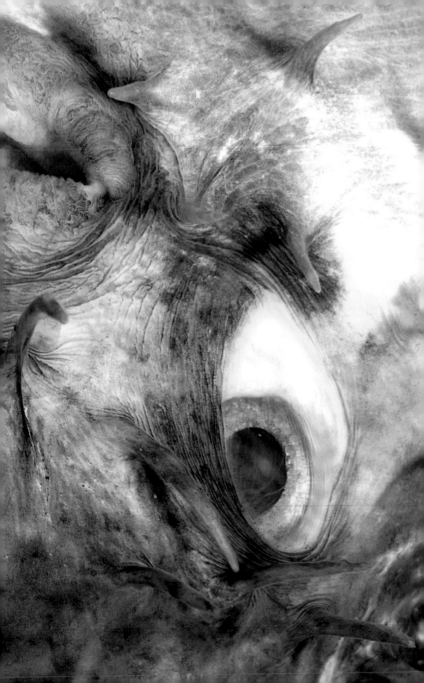

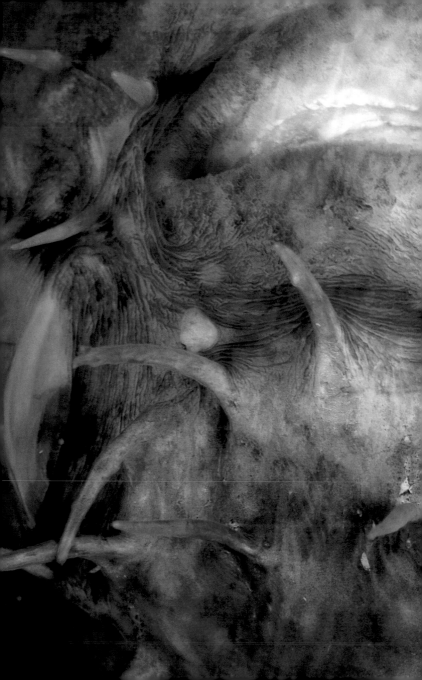

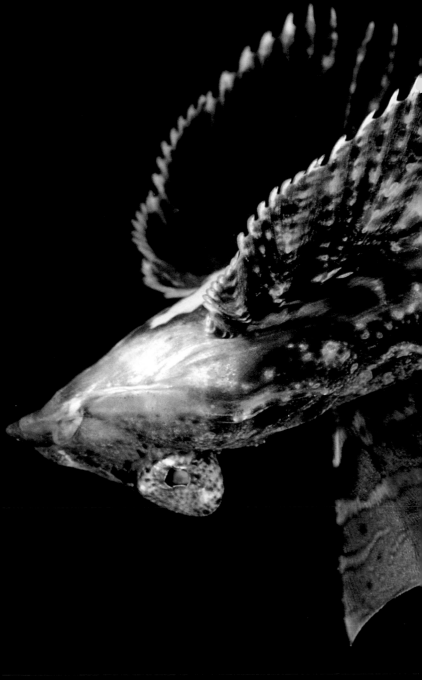

Dragonet fish, Suruga Bay, Japan, 1989
Overleaf: Nassau grouper and Cleaner goby,
Cayo Largo, Cuba, 2000

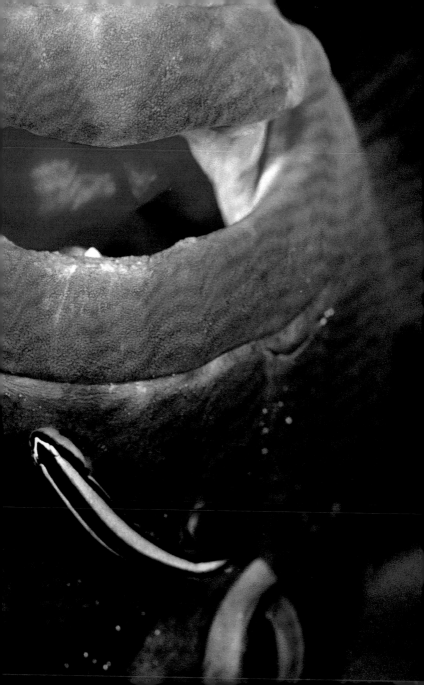

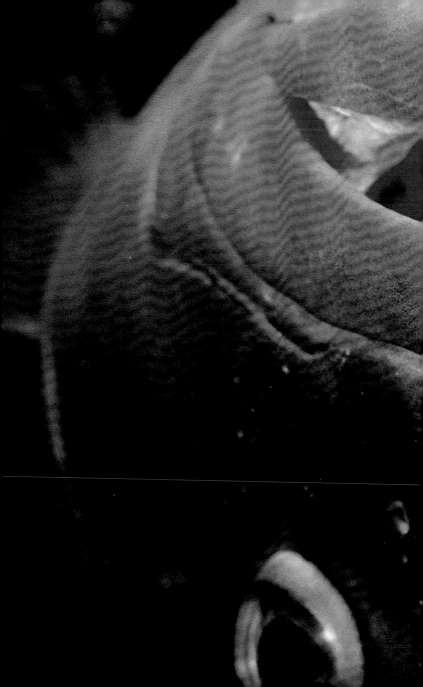

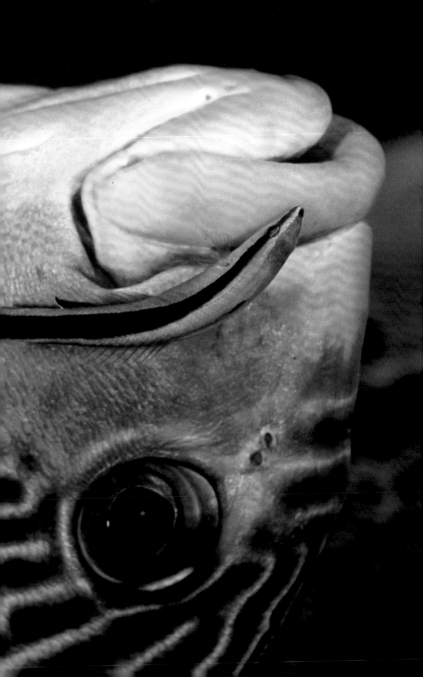

Diagonal-banded sweetlips and Cleaner wrasse,
Bali, Indonesia, 1996
Overleaf: Nine-lined sweetlips, Aldabra Atoll,
Seychelles, 1992

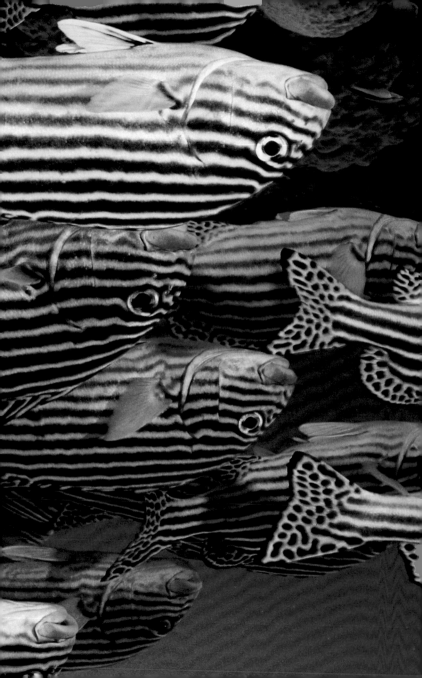

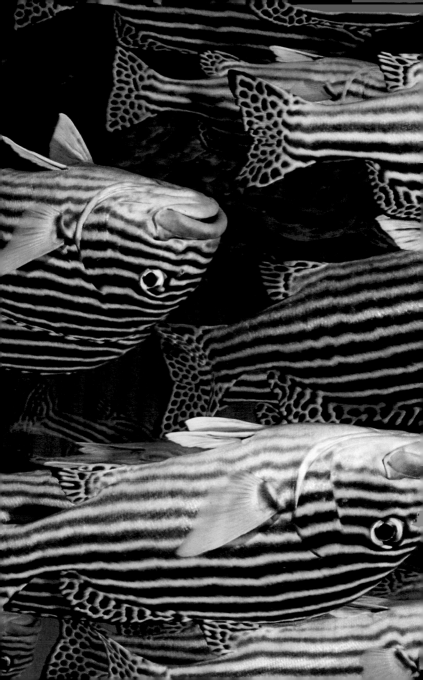

Longfin batfish, Sipadan Island, Malaysia, 1996

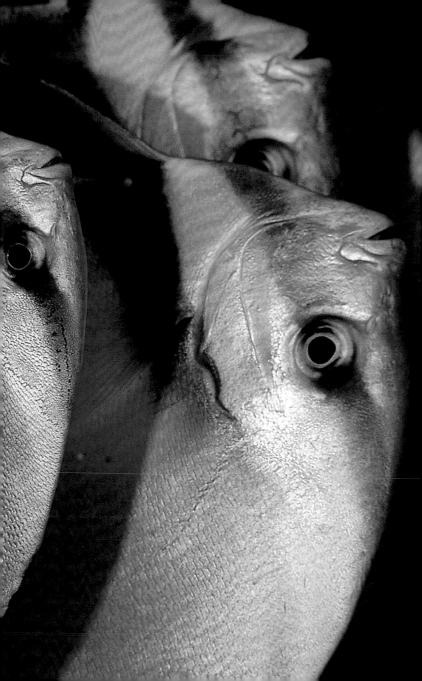

Inimicus scorpion fish, Kungkungan Bay,
Indonesia, 2001
Overleaf: Inimicus scorpion fish, Kungkungan Bay,
Indonesia, 2001

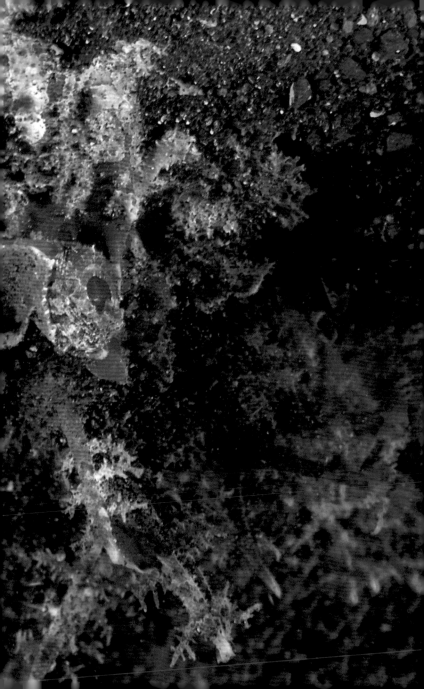

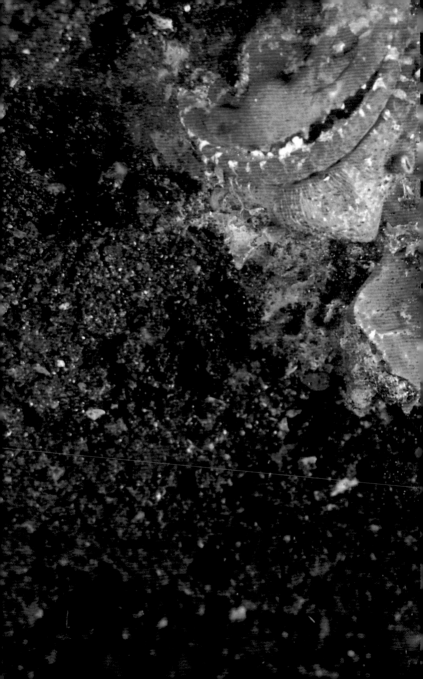

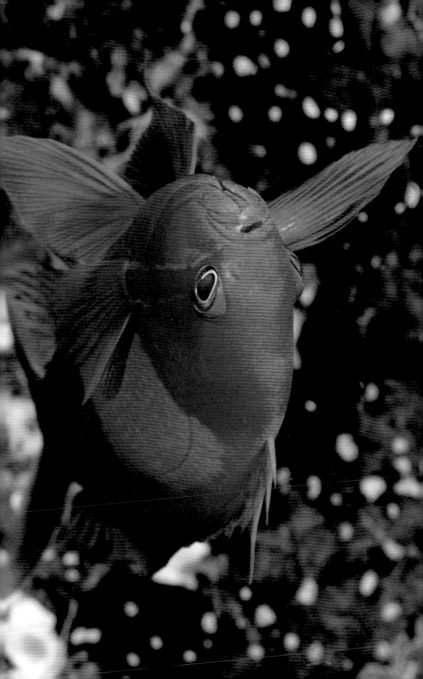

Squarespot anthias, German Channel, Palau, 1996
Overleaf: Orangespine unicorn fish, Milne Bay,
Papua New Guinea, 1996

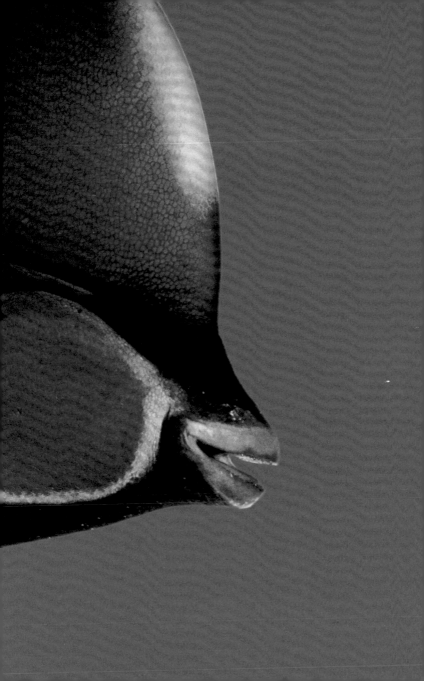

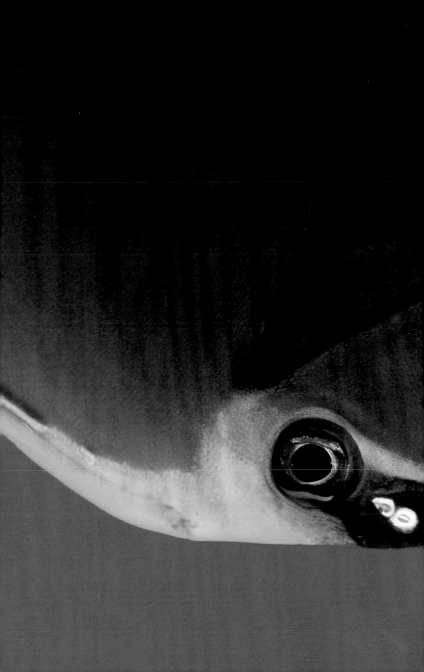

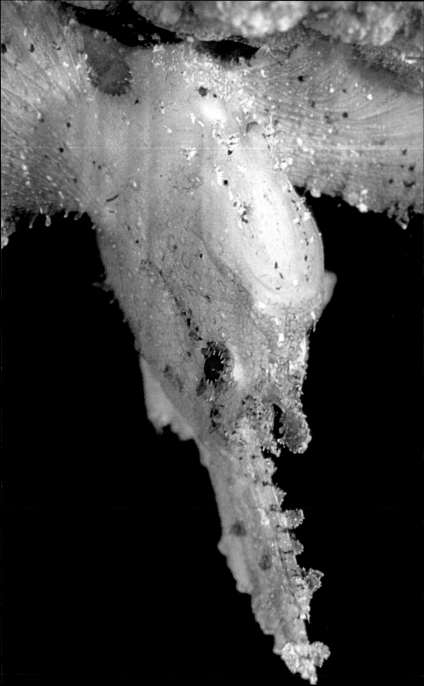

Leaf scorpion fish, Manado, Indonesia, 1995
Overleaf: Spotted scorpion fish, Lighthouse Reef,
Belize, 2002

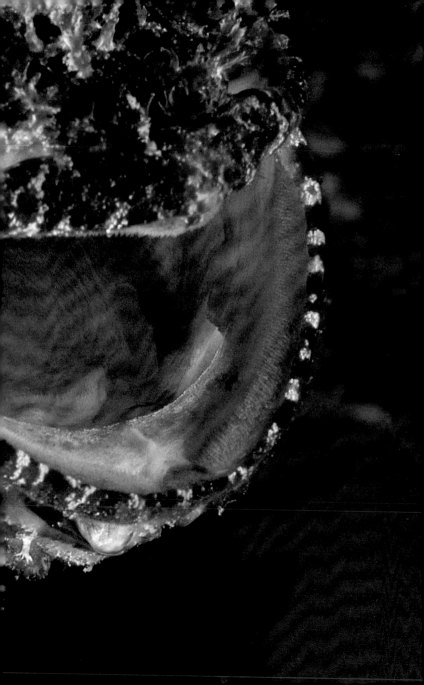

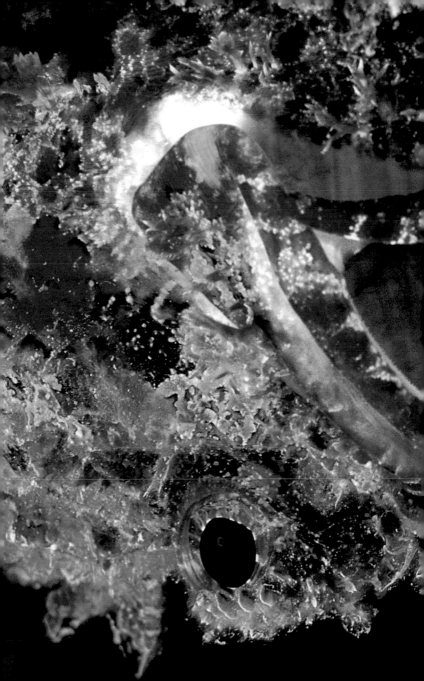

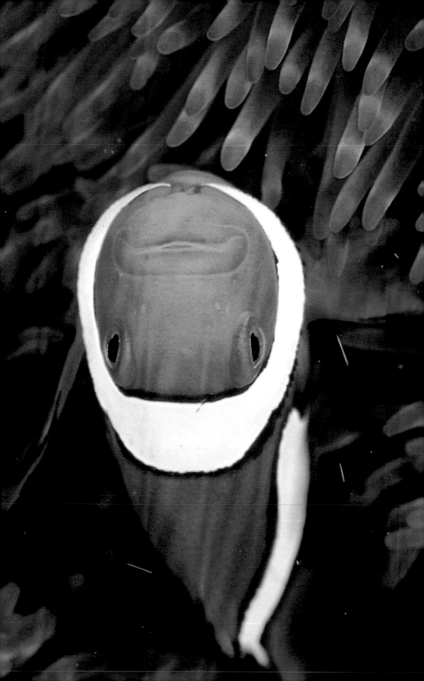

Clown anemone fish, Milne Bay,
Papua New Guinea, 1996
Overleaf: Blue triggerfish and Cleaner wrasse,
Red Sea, Israel, 1977

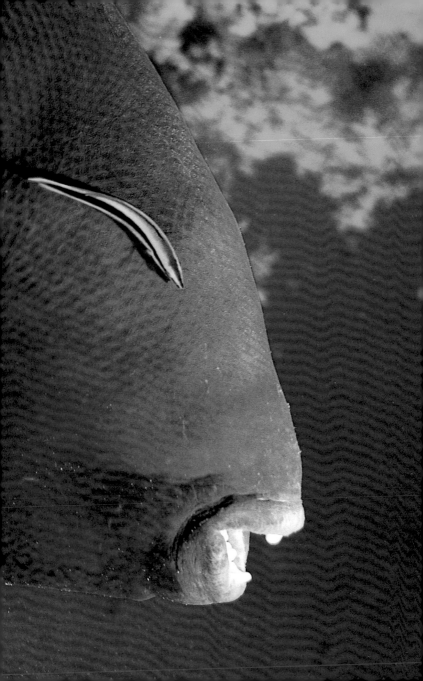

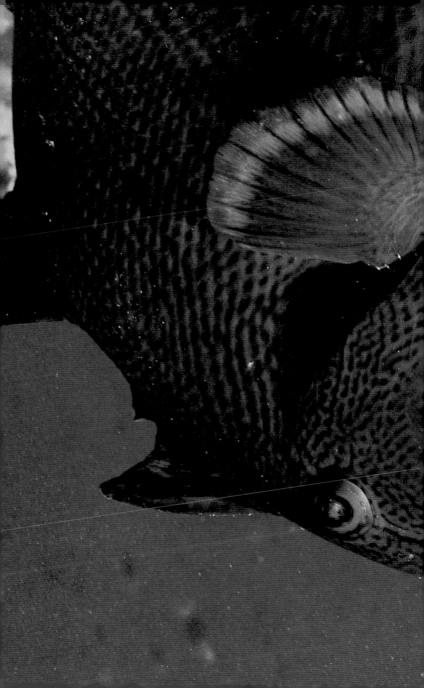

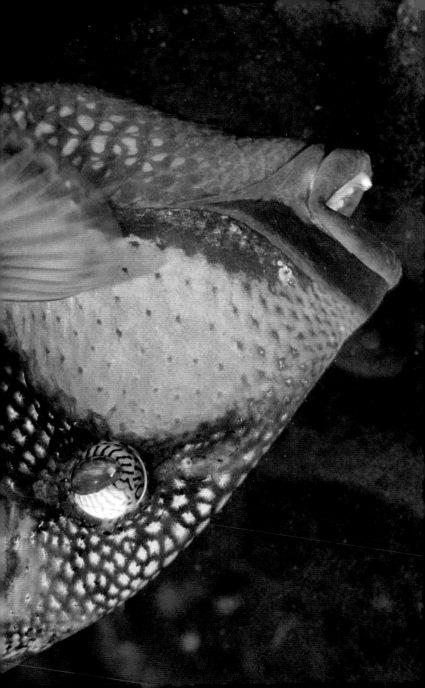

Titan trigger fish, Red Sea, Israel, 1985
Overleaf: Whale shark, North Cape,
Western Australia, 1992

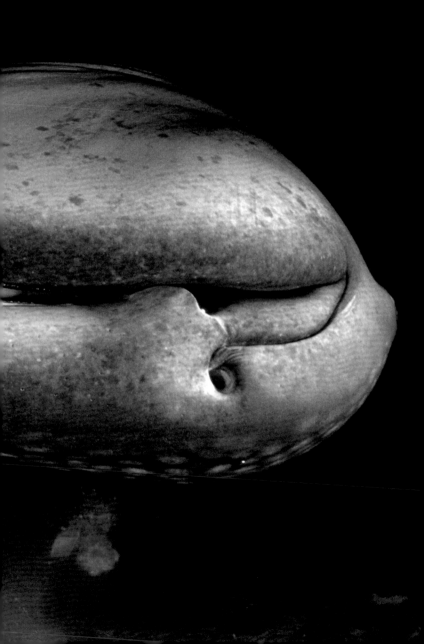

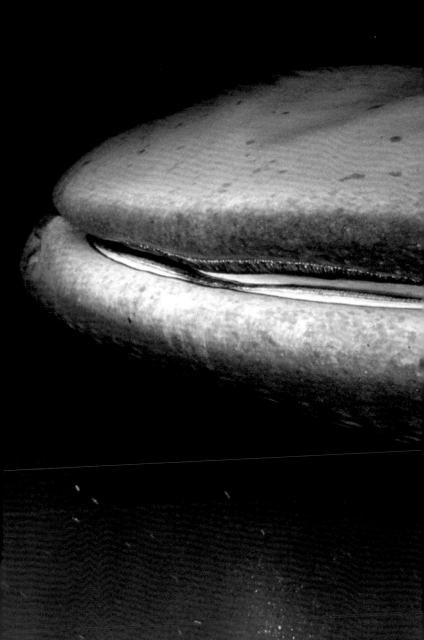

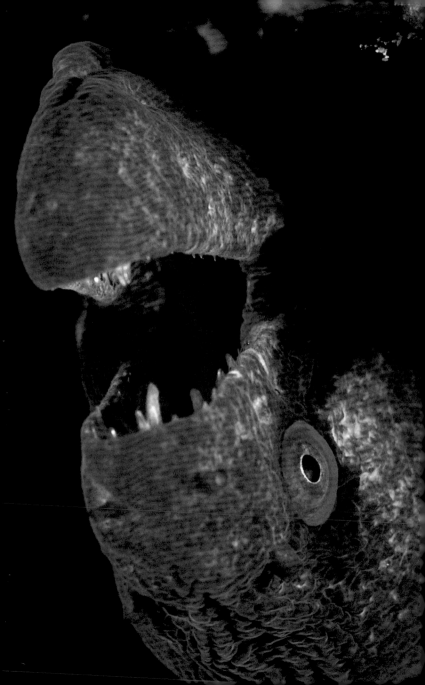

Hawk-faced moray eel, Astove Atoll, Seychelles, 1993
Overleaf: Great barracuda, Little Cayman Island, 1999

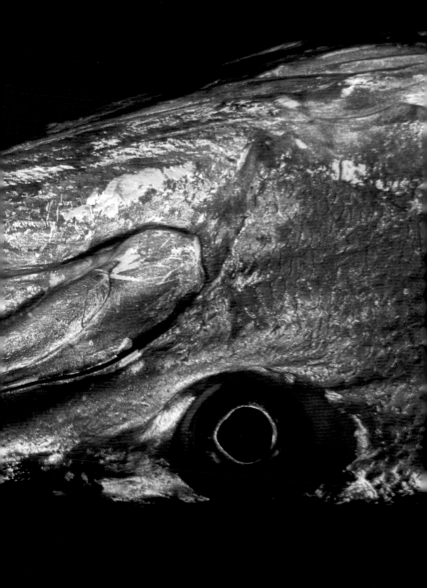

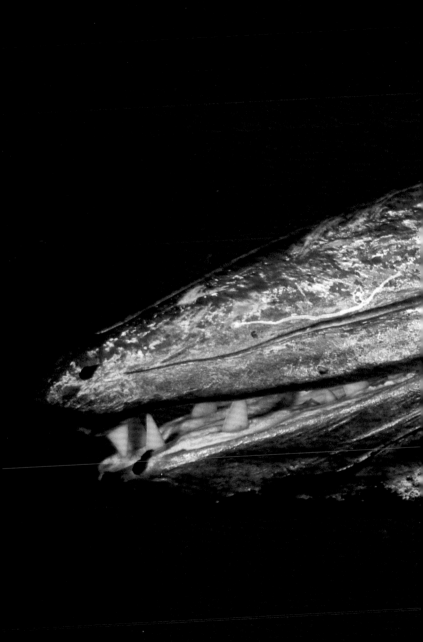

Tarpon, Grand Cayman Island, 1999

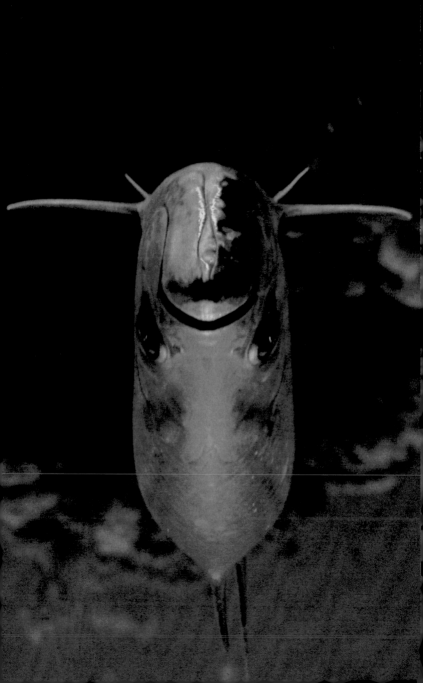

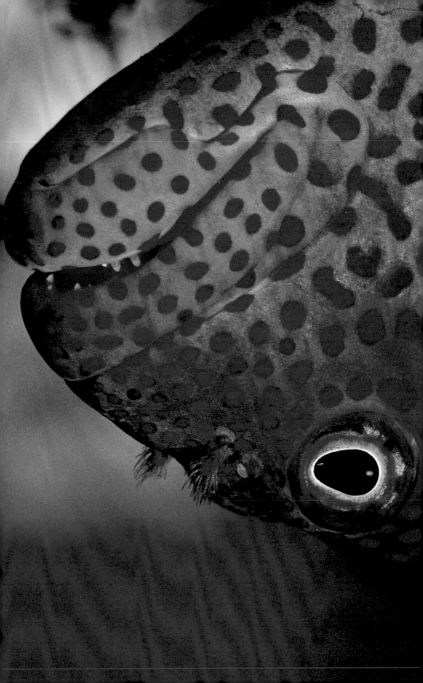

Red-spotted hawk fish, Hawaii, USA, 1985
Overleaf: Manta ray, Hawaii, USA, 1994

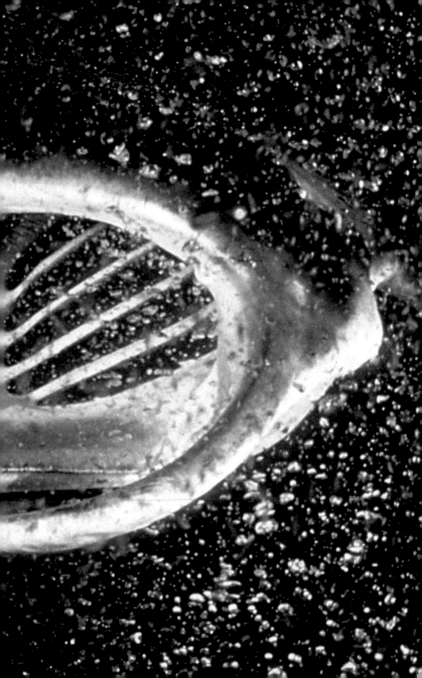

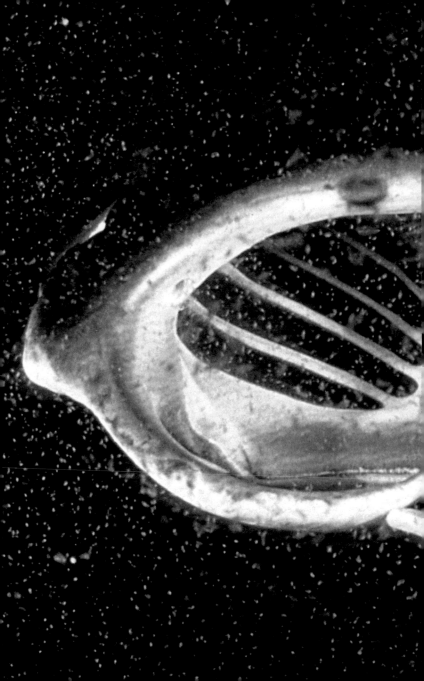

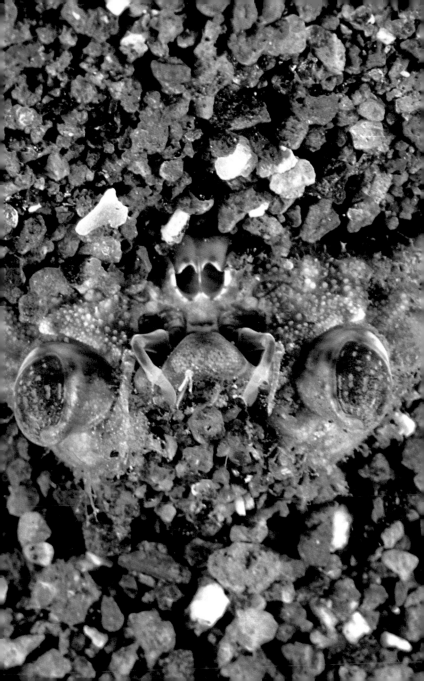

Box crab, Saba, Netherlands Antilles, 2002
Overleaf: Stargazer, Red Sea, Israel, 1981

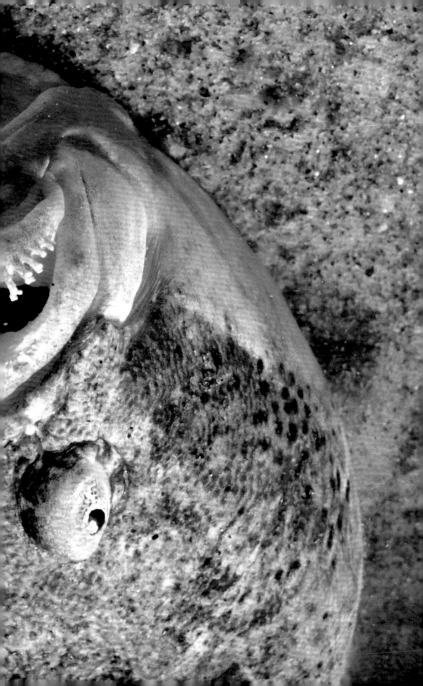

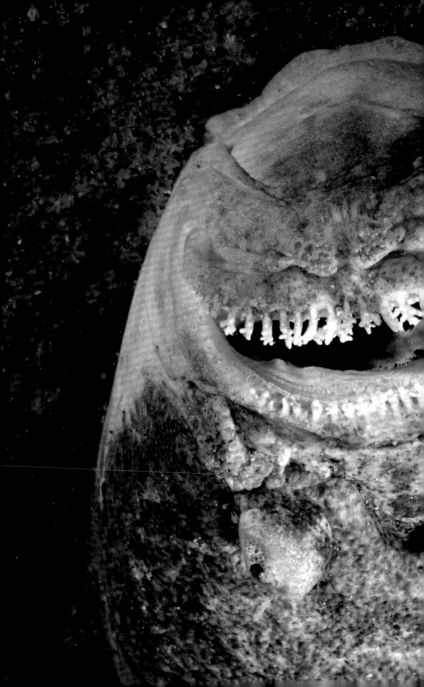

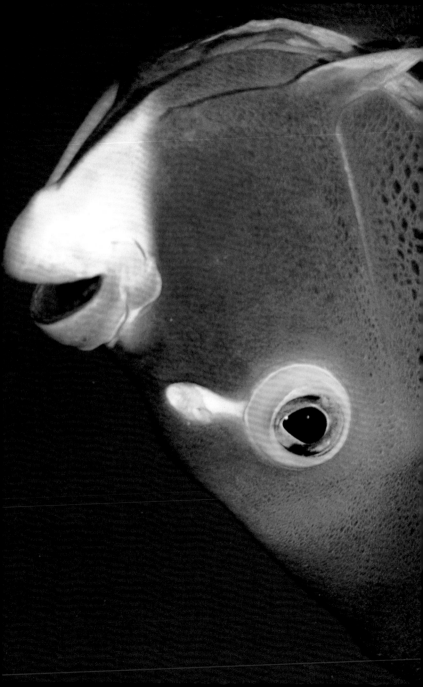

French angel fish, Grand Cayman Island, 1985
Overleaf: French angel fish, Grand Cayman Island, 1985

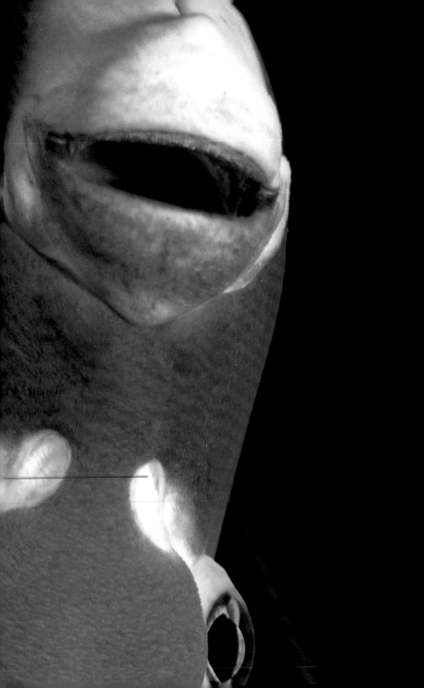

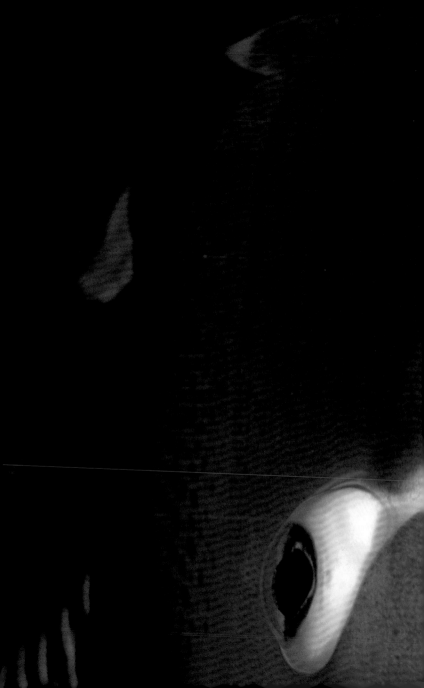

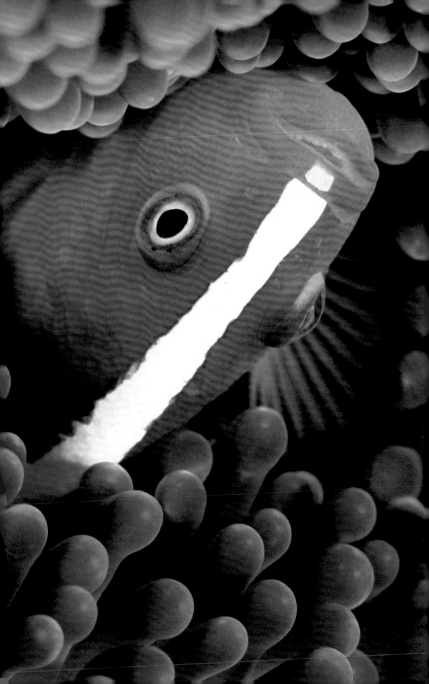

Orange anemone fish, Russell Islands,
Solomon Islands, 1986
Overleaf: Sculpin, Tasmania, Australia, 1995

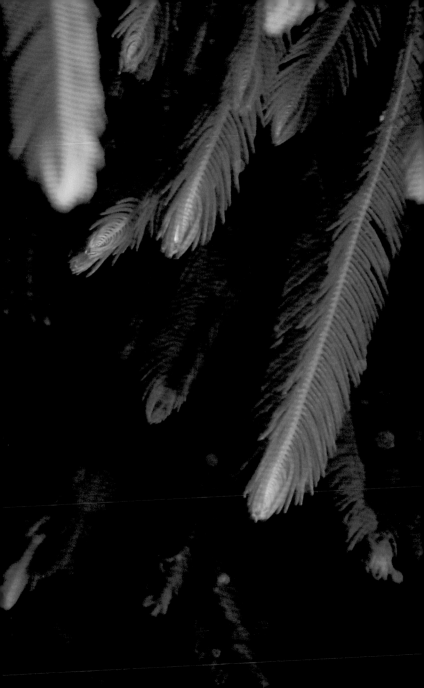

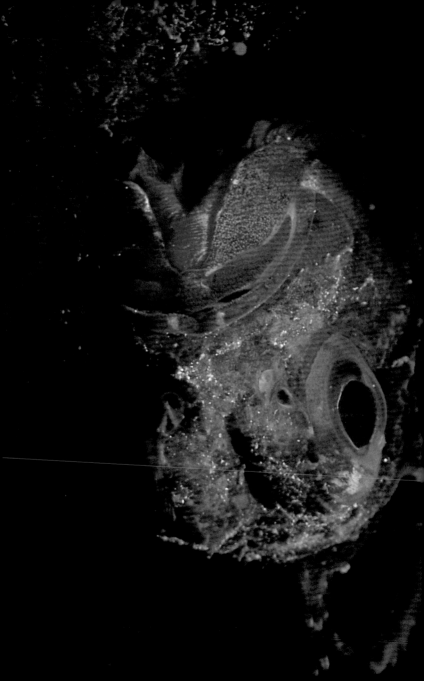

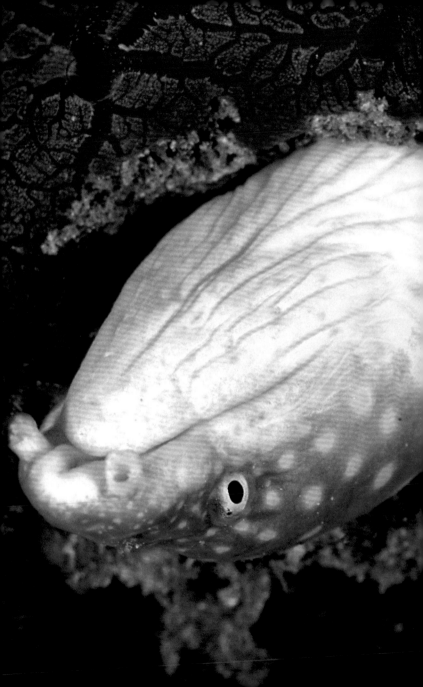

Sharp-tailed snake eel, St Lucia, 1979
Overleaf: Star puffer fish, Bora Bora,
French Polynesia, 1995

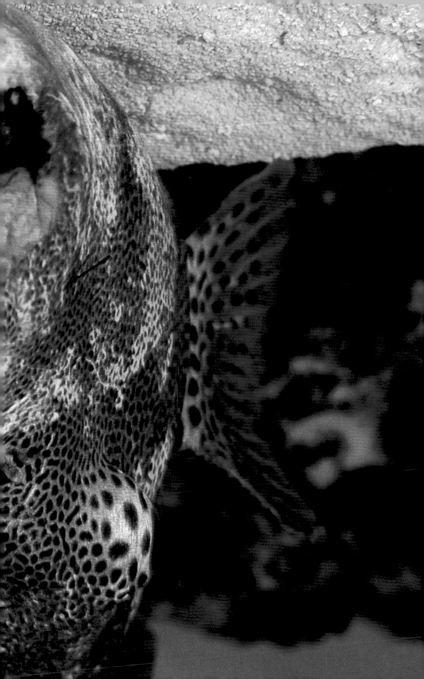

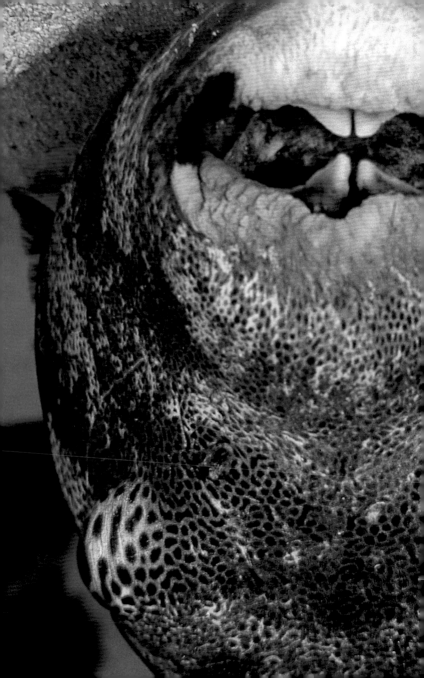

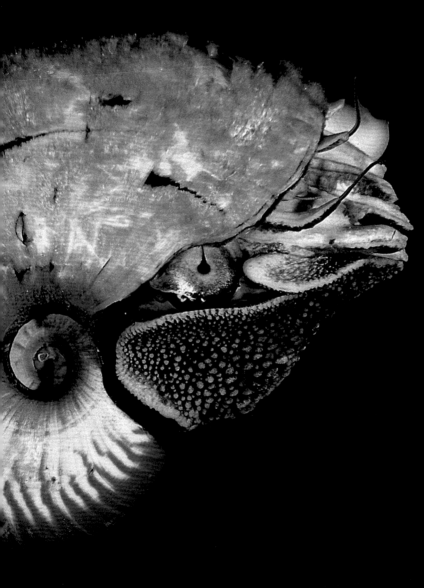

Chambered nautilus, Manus Island,
Papua New Guinea, 1987
Overleaf: Lizard fish, Bali, Indonesia, 1996

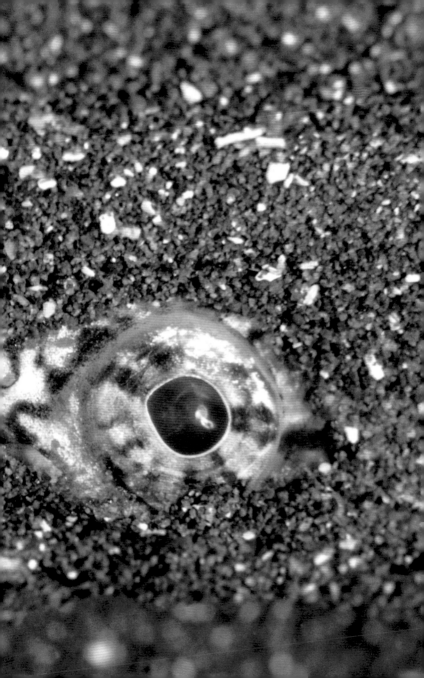

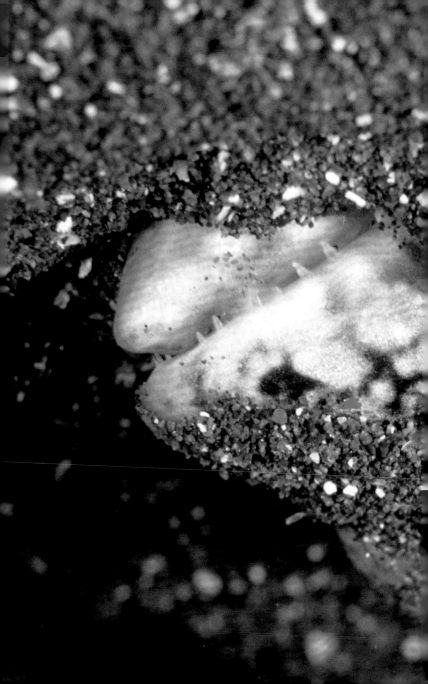

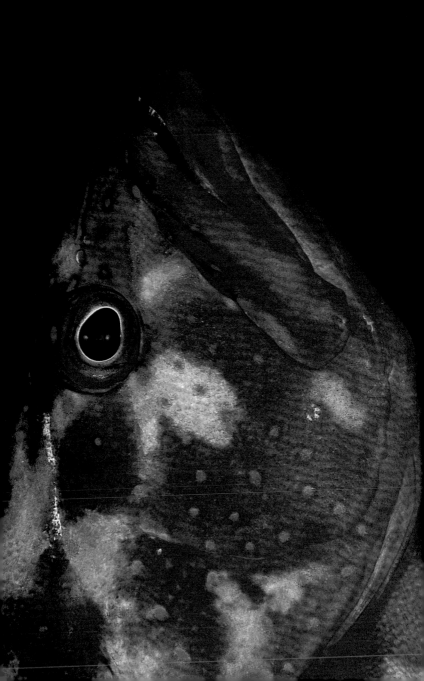

Blue-spotted grouper, Kimbe Bay,
Papua New Guinea, 1996
Overleaf: Banded goby, Flores, Indonesia, 1996

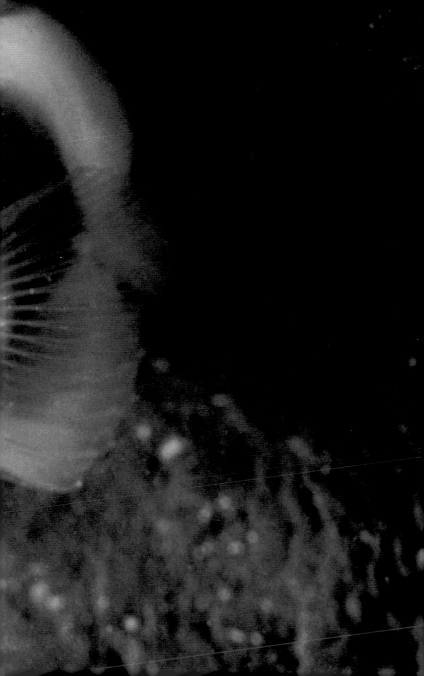

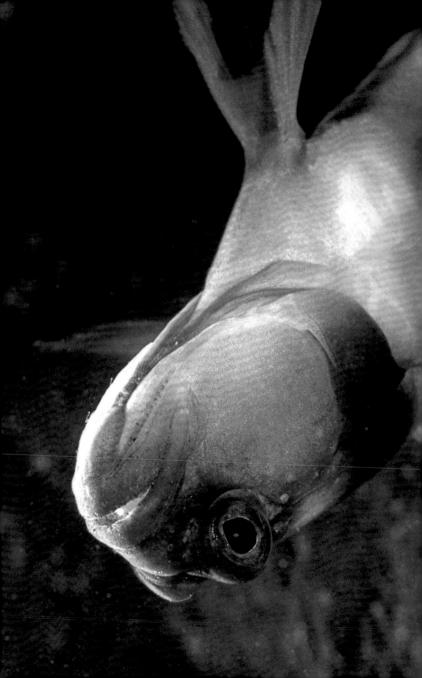

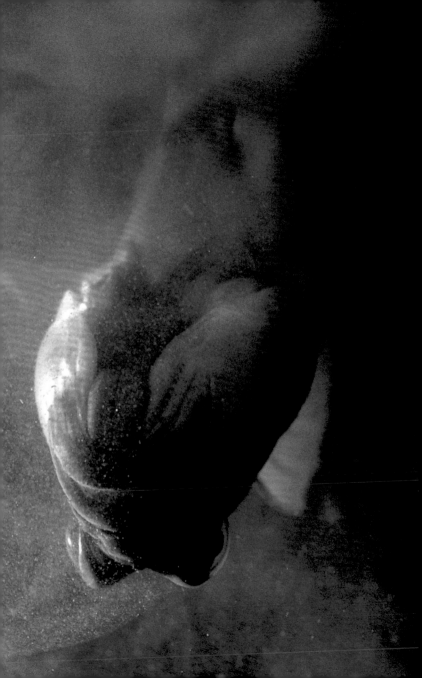

Banded goby, Flores, Indonesia, 1
Overleaf: Cabezon, Monterey, Cali

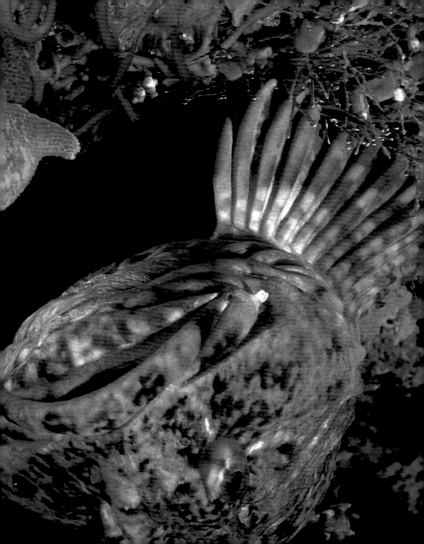

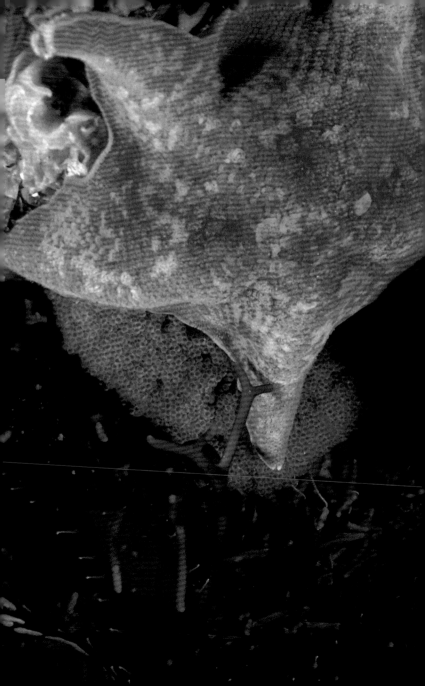

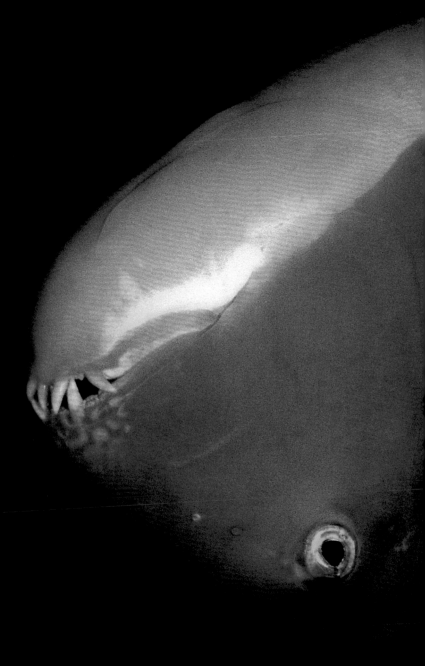

Venus (anchor) tusk fish, Great Barrier Reef,
Australia, 1999
Overleaf: Japanese scorpion fish, Izu, Japan, 1981

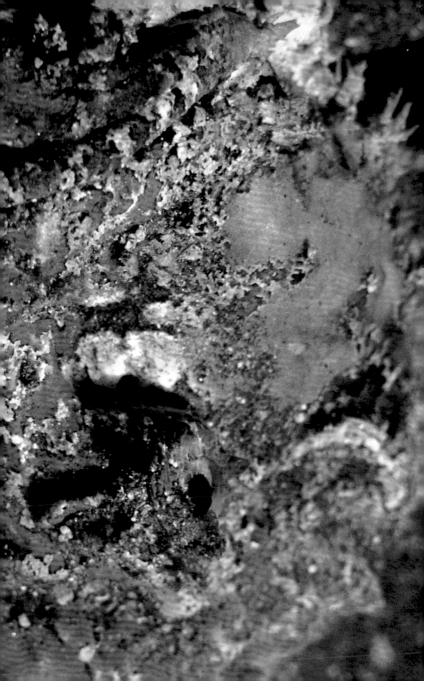

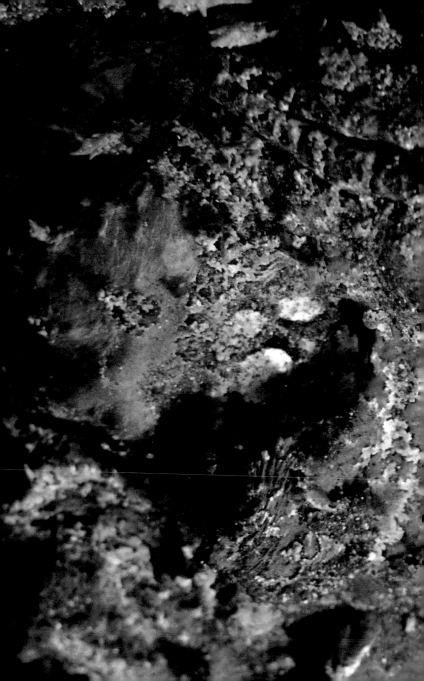

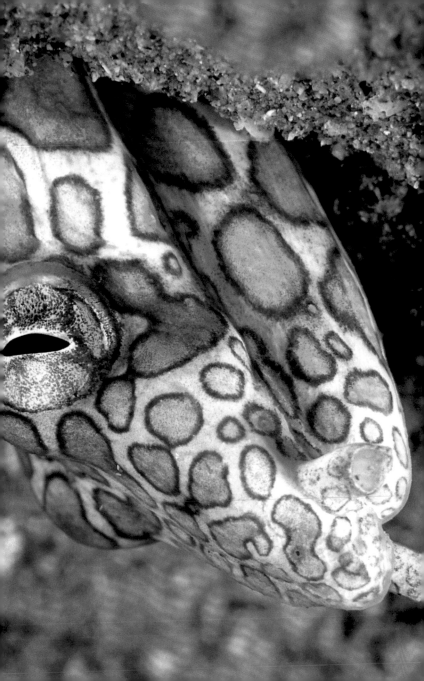

Clown snake eel, Bali, Indonesia, 1996
Overleaf: Jew fish, Grand Cayman Island, 1986

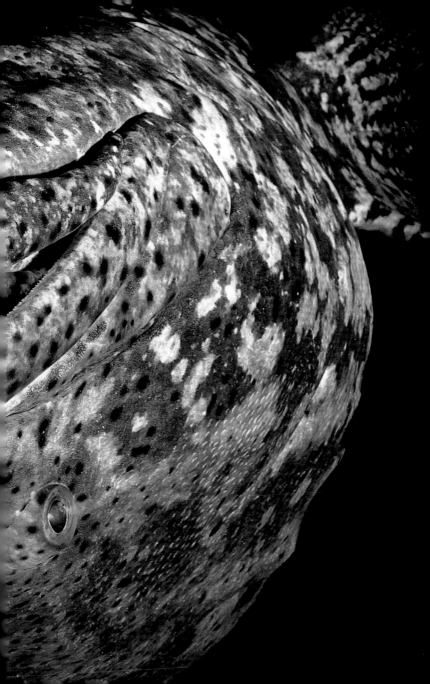

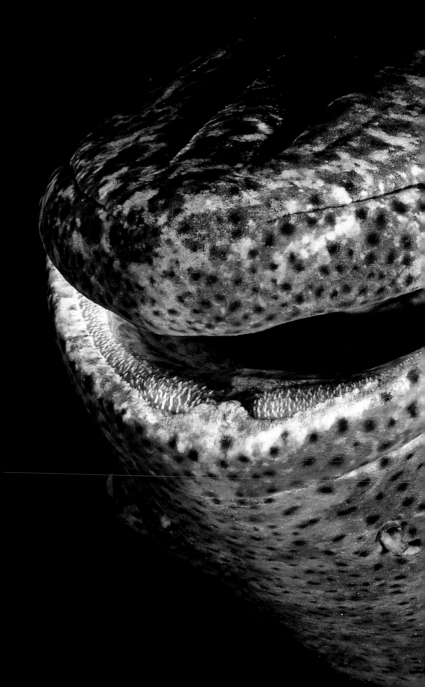

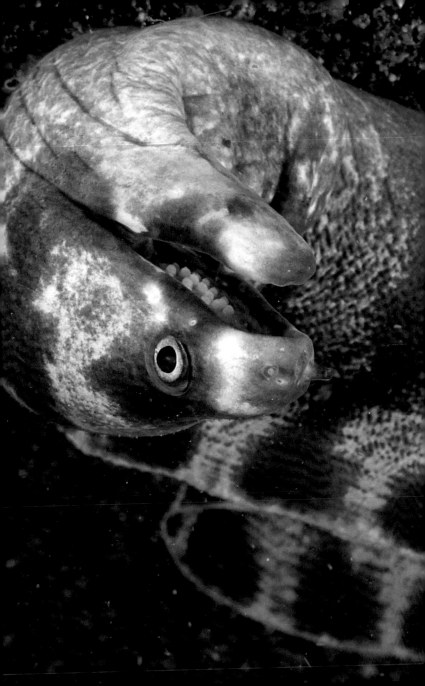

Mottled moray eel, Kungkungan Bay, Indonesia, 2001
Overleaf: Red Sea coral grouper, Brothers Islands,
Egypt, 1991

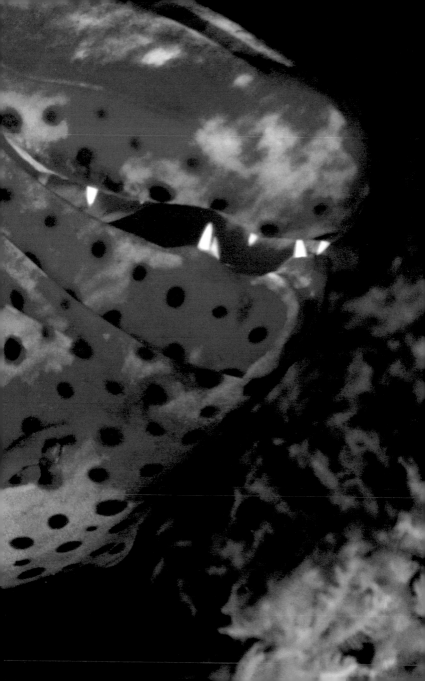

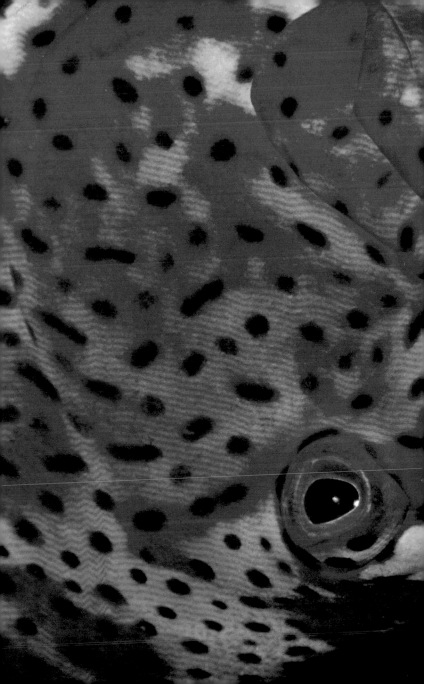

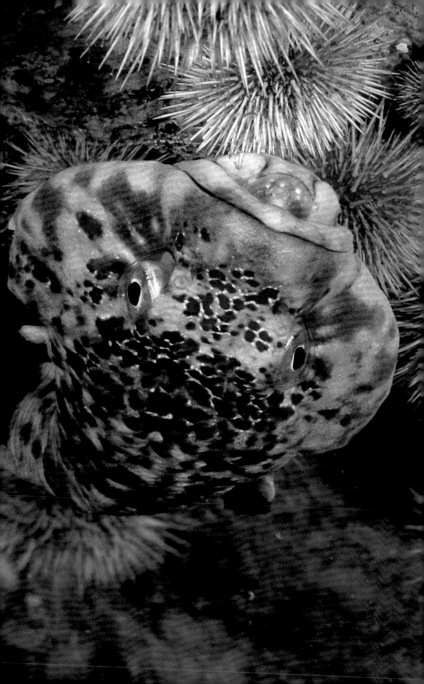

Urchin puffer fish, False Bay, South Africa, 2001
Overleaf: Octopus, False Bay, South Africa, 2001

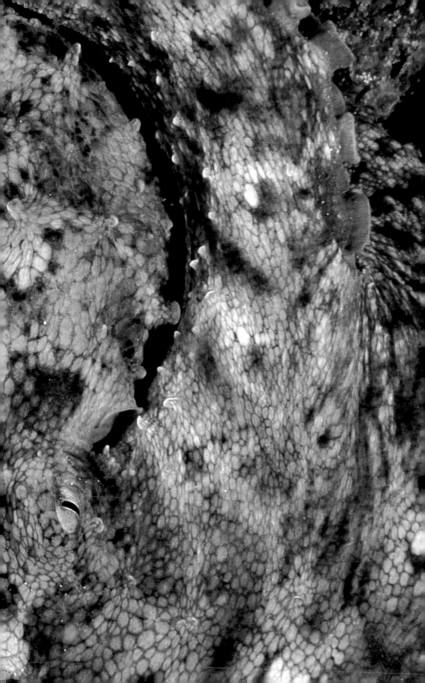

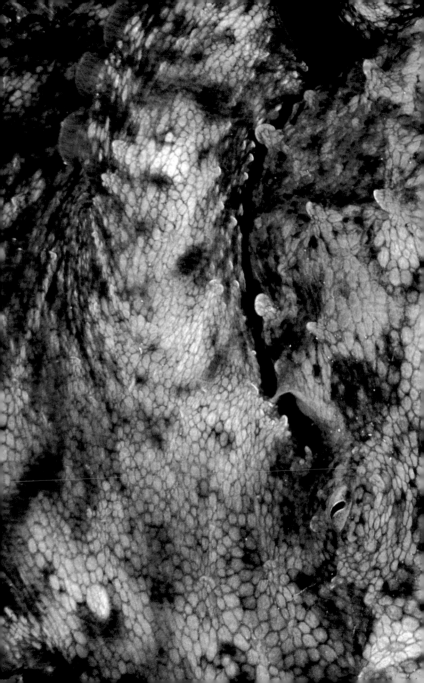

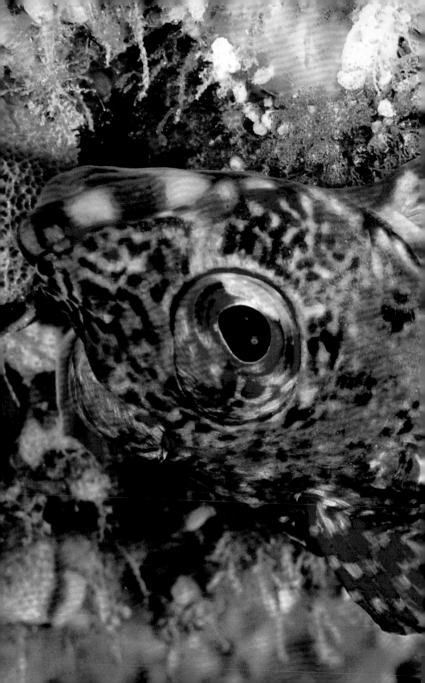

Hotlips tripplefin, False Bay, South Africa, 2001
Overleaf: Blue shark, California, USA, 1979

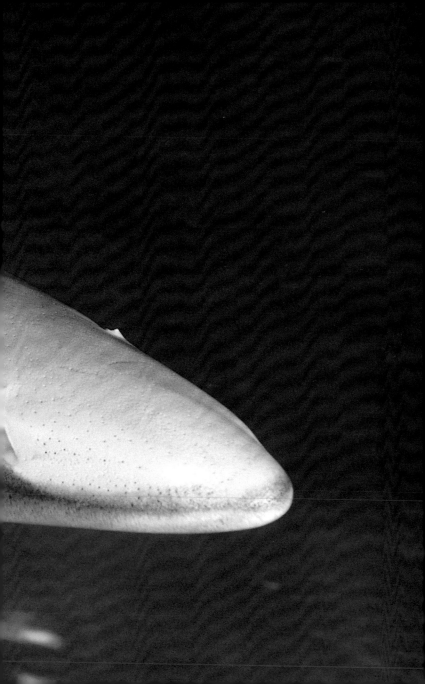

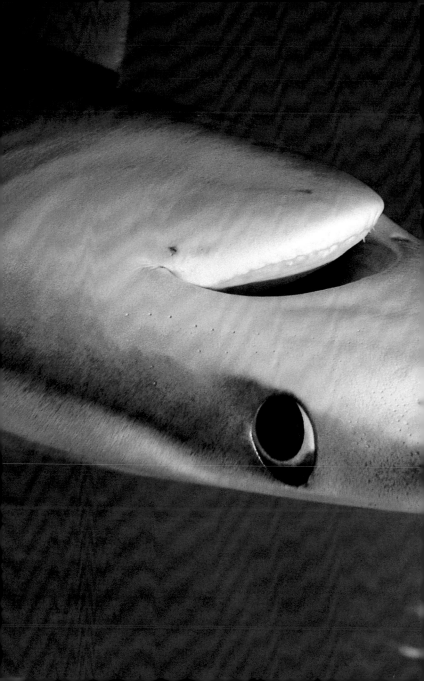

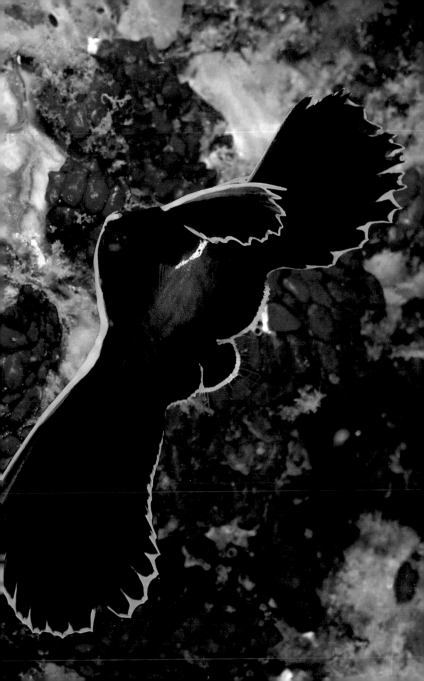

Pinnate bat fish, Kungkungan Bay, Indonesia, 2001
Overleaf: Barbed-mouth fish, False Bay,
South Africa, 2001

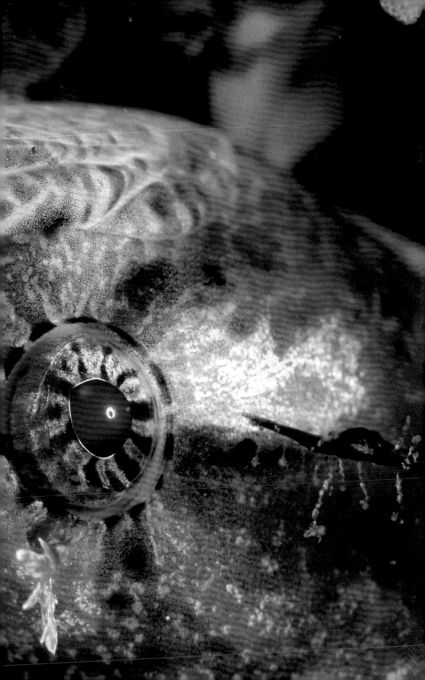

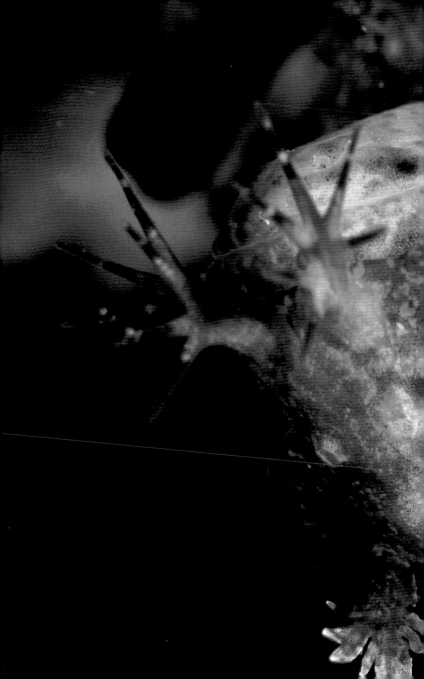

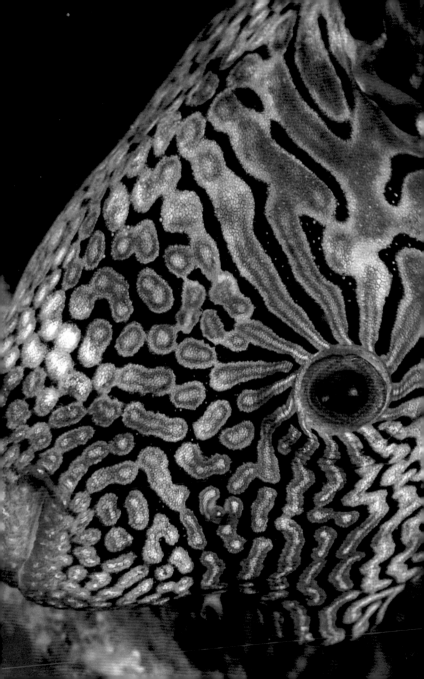

Map puffer fish, Great Barrier Reef, Australia, 1999
Overleaf: Stars and stripes puffer fish and Shrimp,
Great Barrier Reef, Australia, 1999

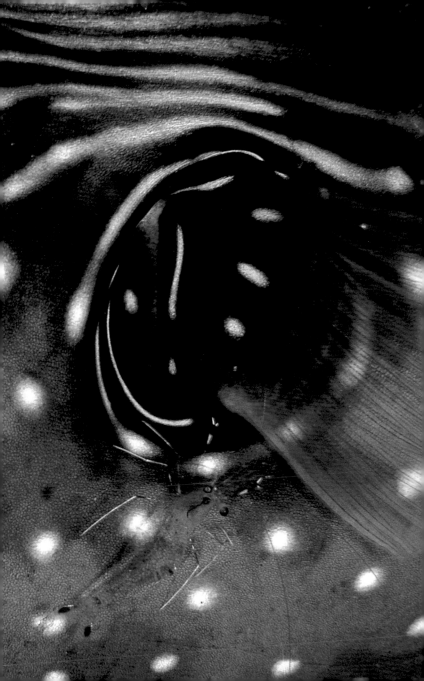

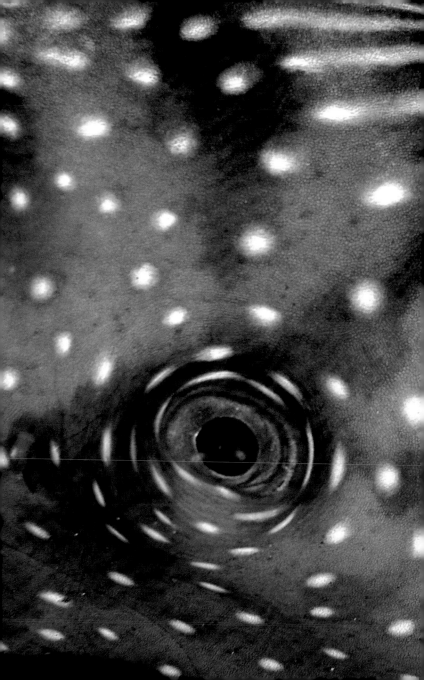

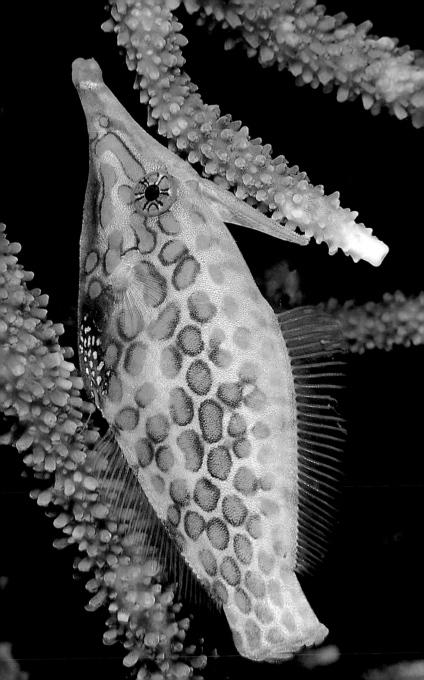

Beaked leather jacket, Kungkungan Bay,
Indonesia, 2001
Overleaf: Reef squid, Isle of Youth, Cuba, 2000

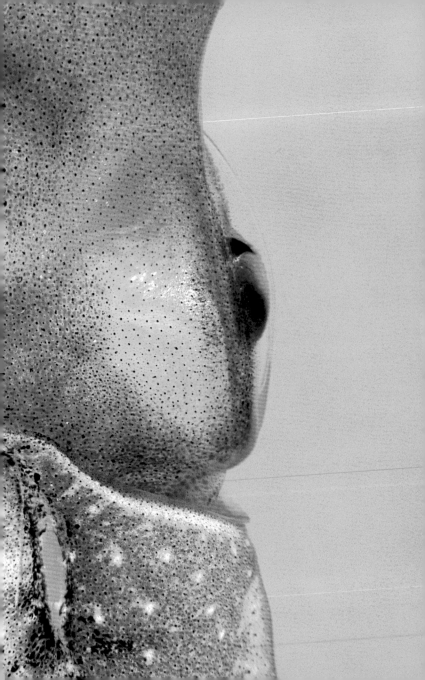

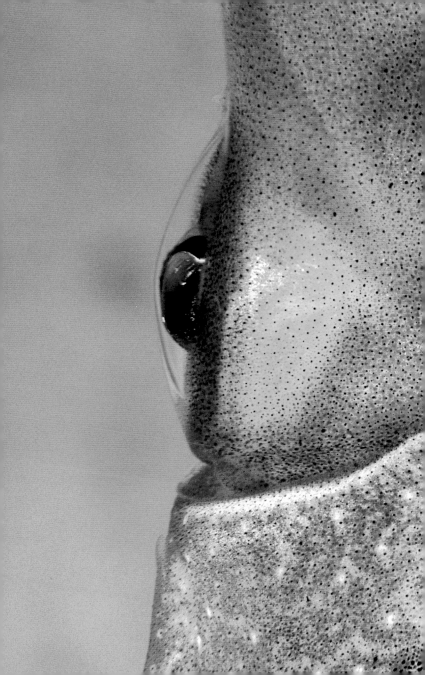

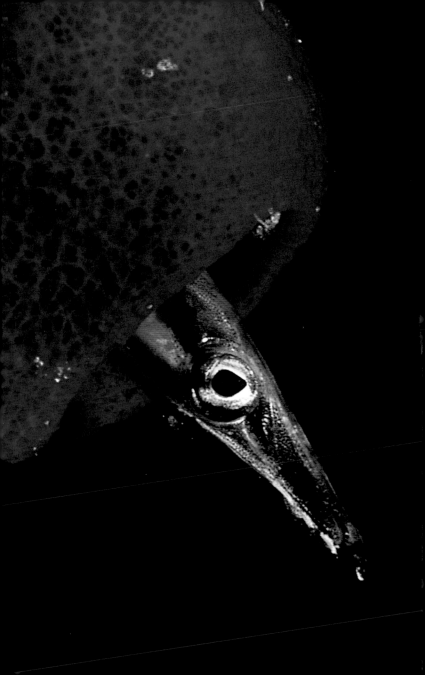

Pike blenny, Cayo Largo, Cuba, 2000
Overleaf: Slipper lobster, Kungkungan Bay,
Indonesia, 2001

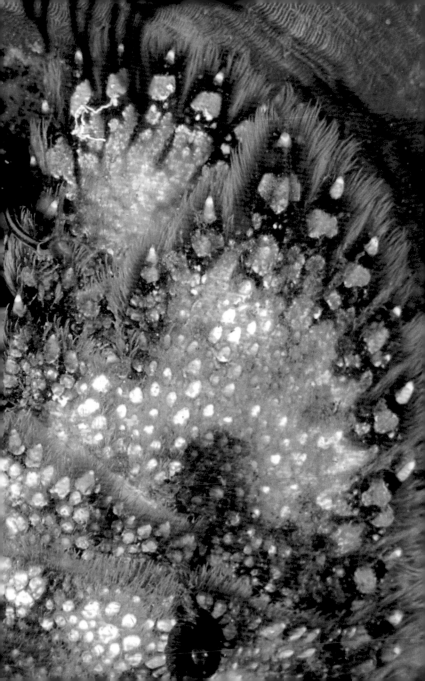

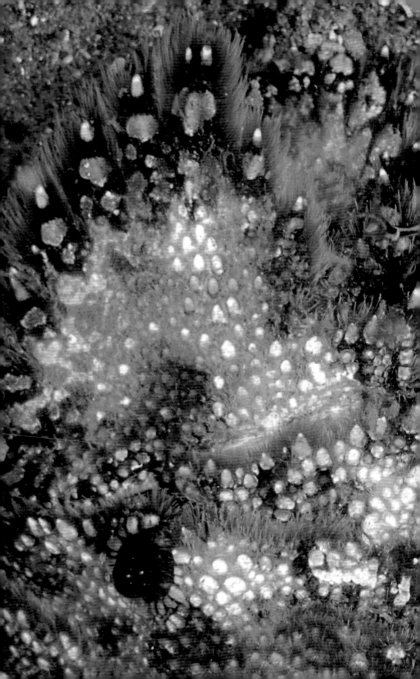

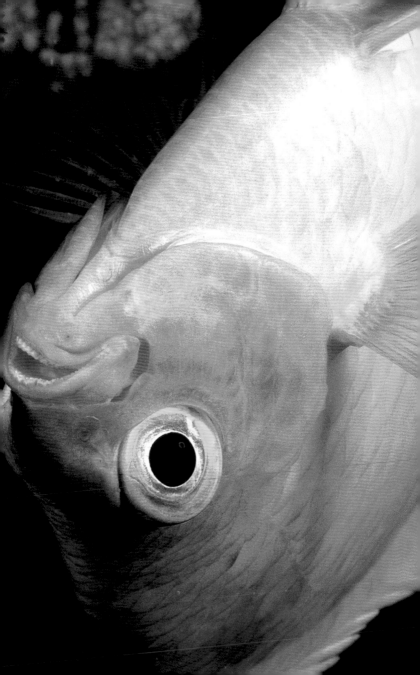

Yellow damsel fish, Great Barrier Reef, Australia, 1999

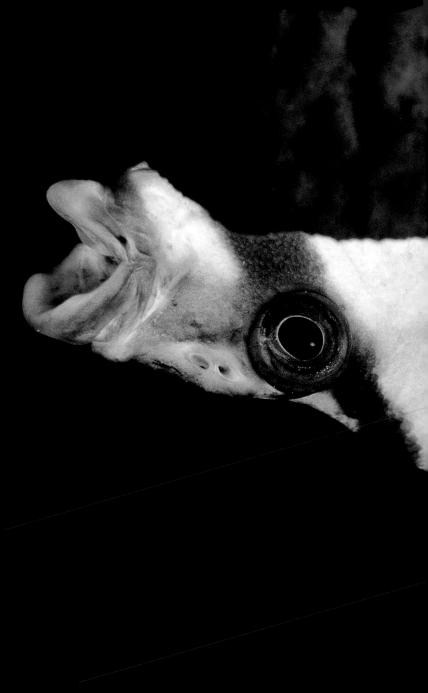

Striped morwong, South Australia, 1984
Overleaf: Morwong, Lord Howe Island, Australia, 1987

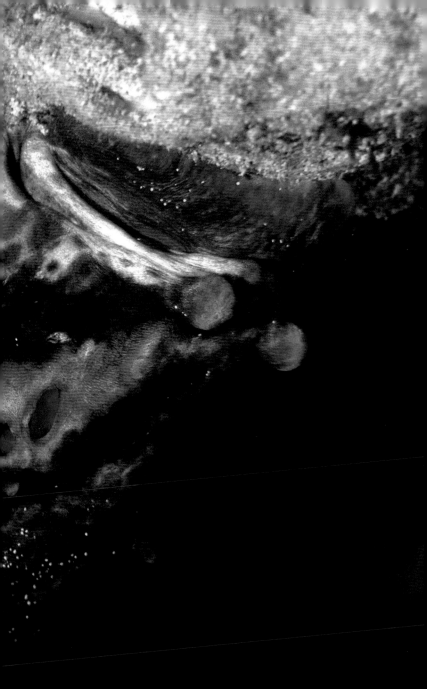

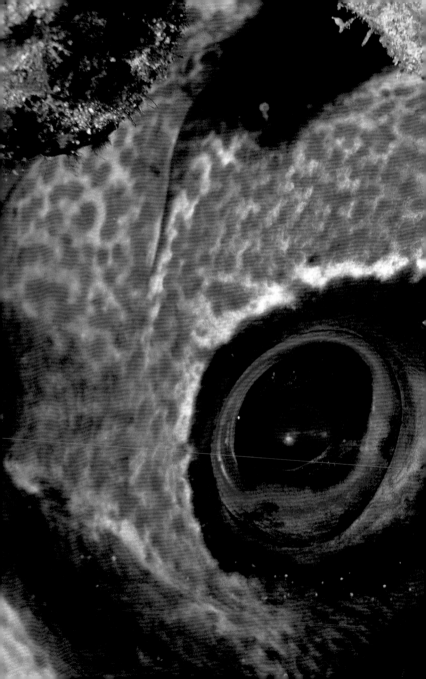

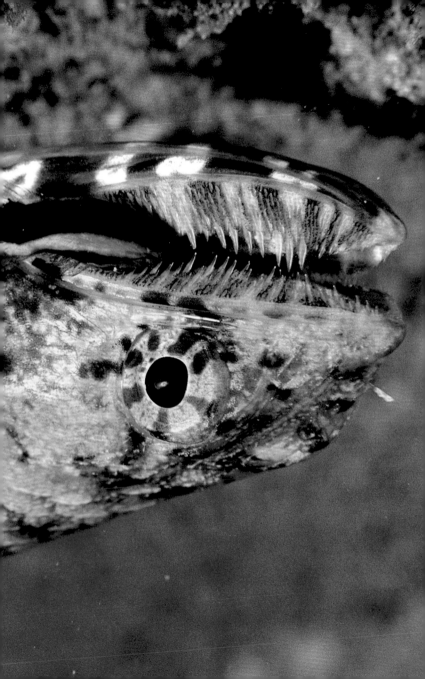

Lizard fish eating a False cleaner wrasse,
Espirito Santo Island, Vanuatu, 1986
Overleaf: Stoplight parrot fish in sleeping bubble,
Grand Cayman Island, 1984

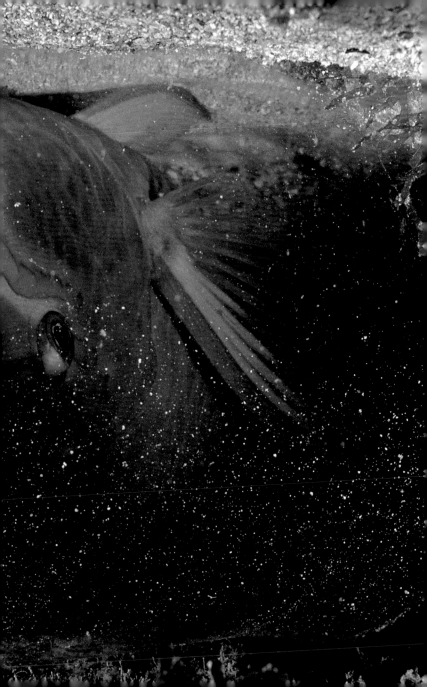

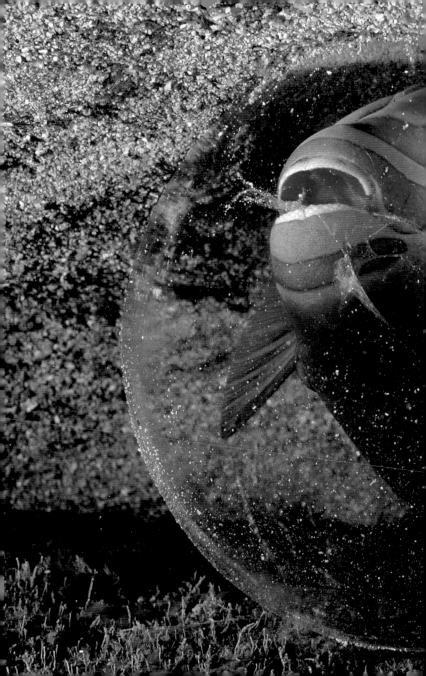

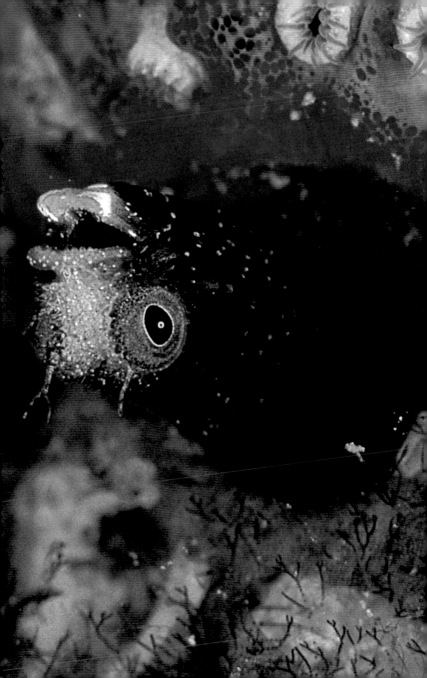

Spinyhead blenny, Cayo Largo, Cuba, 2000
Overleaf: Great white shark, Gansbaai,
South Africa, 1999

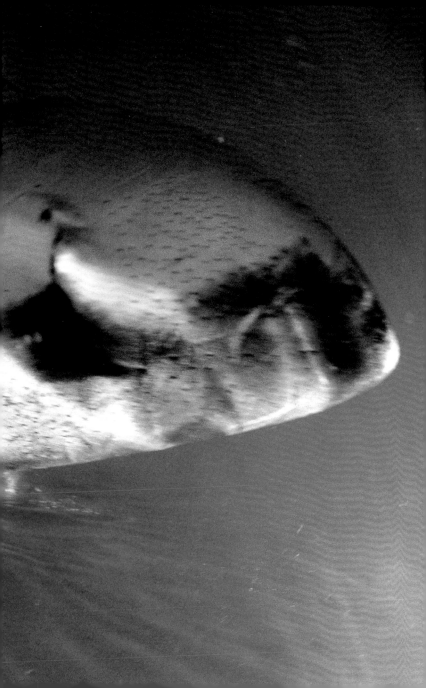

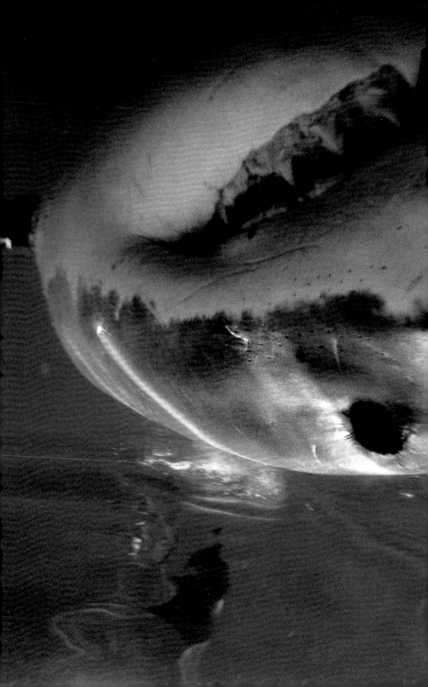

Great white shark, Gansbaai, South Africa, 2001

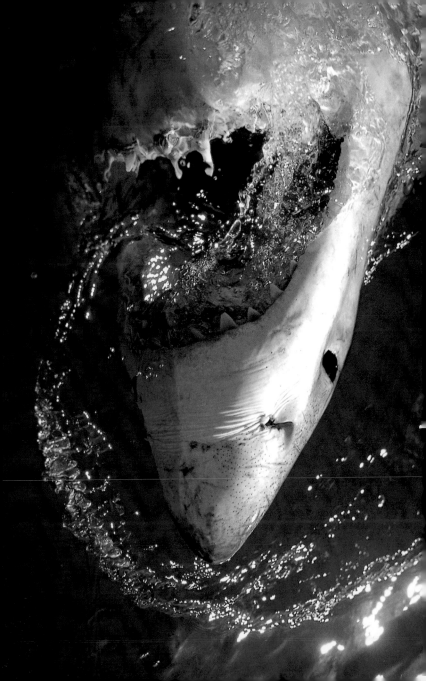

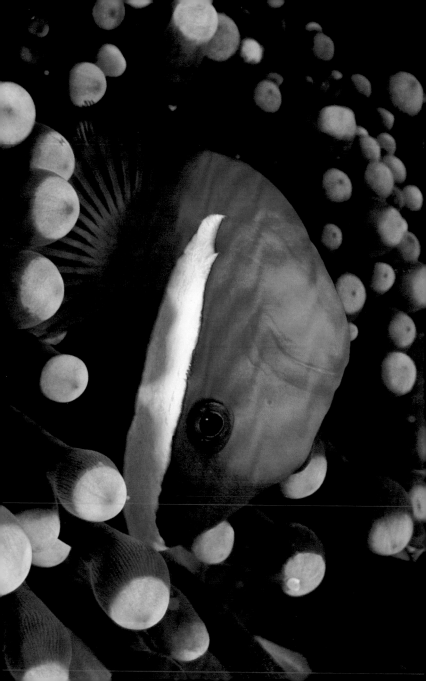

Tomato clown fish, Kimbe Bay,
Papua New Guinea, 1996

Swimmer crab and Shrimp in coral, Mabul, Malaysia, 1996

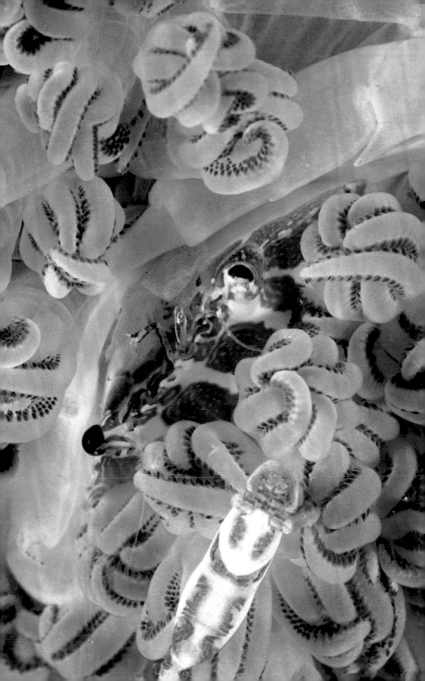

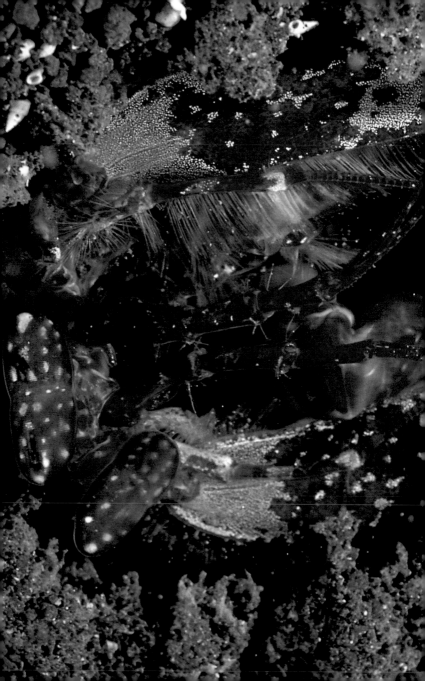

Mantis shrimp, Flores, Indonesia, 1996
Overleaf: Flying gurnard, Kungkungan Bay,
Indonesia, 2001

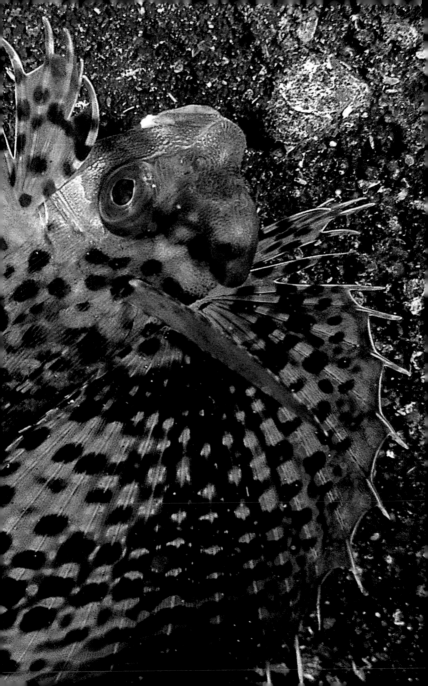

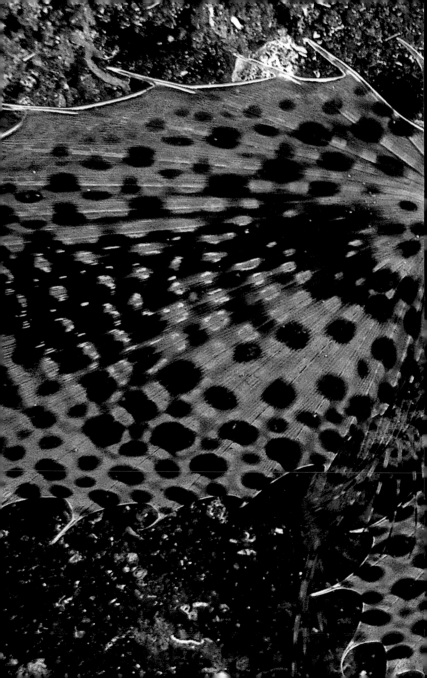

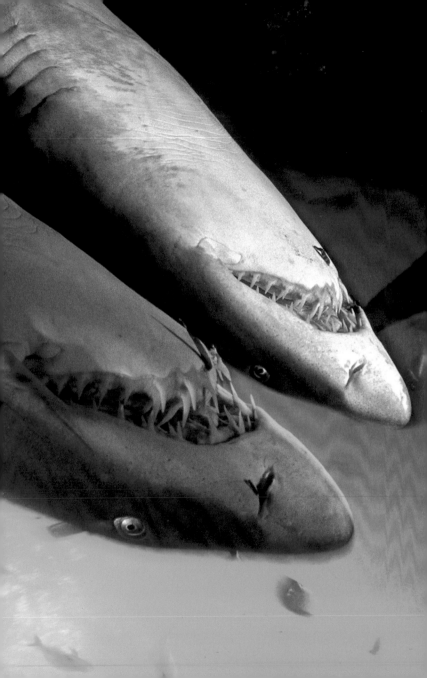

Ragged-tooth sharks, Aliwal Shoals, South Africa, 2001
Overleaf: Ragged-tooth shark, Aliwal Shoals,
South Africa, 2001

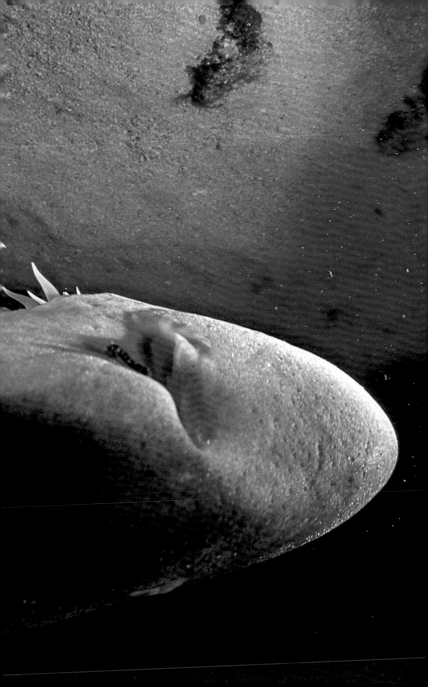

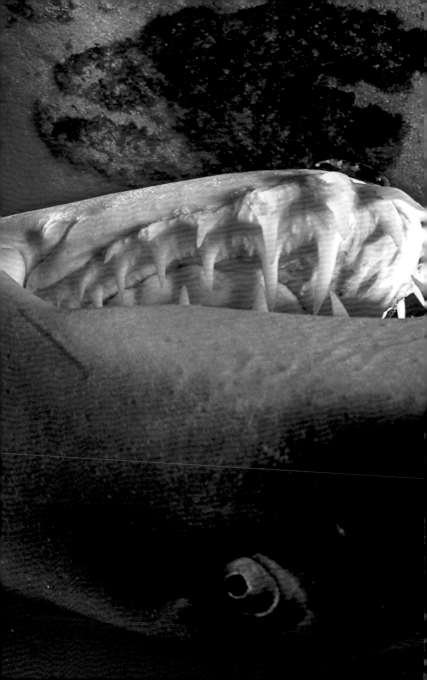

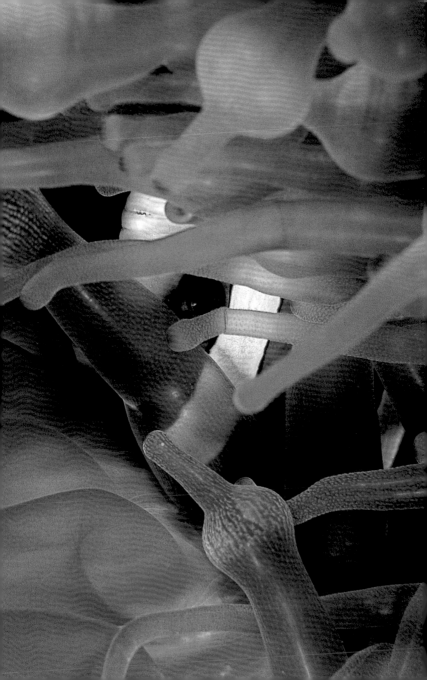

Red and black anemone fish,
Milne Bay, Papua New Guinea, 1996
Overleaf: Southern stingray,
Grand Cayman Island, 1986

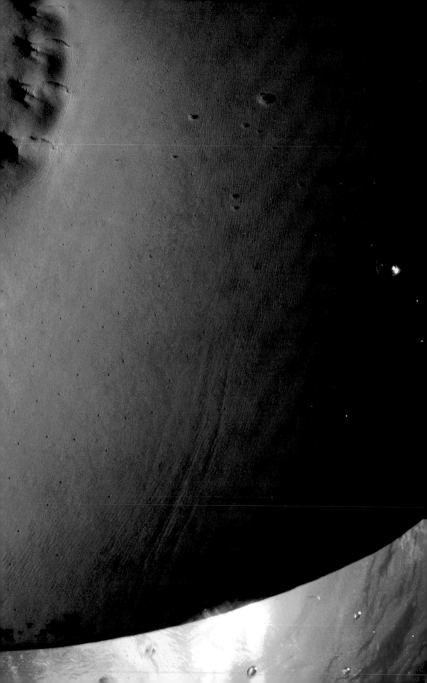

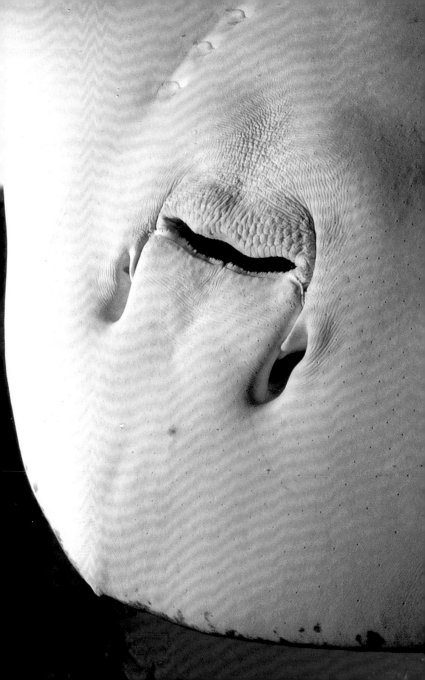

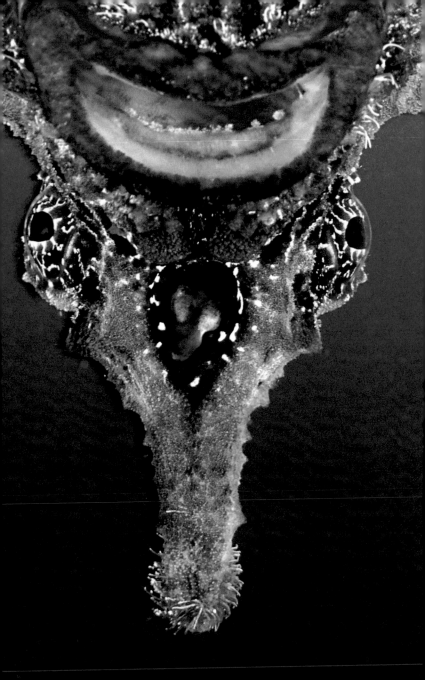

Red-lipped Caribbean batfish, Isle of Youth, Cuba, 2000
Overleaf: Octopus and diver, Cayo Largo, Cuba, 2000

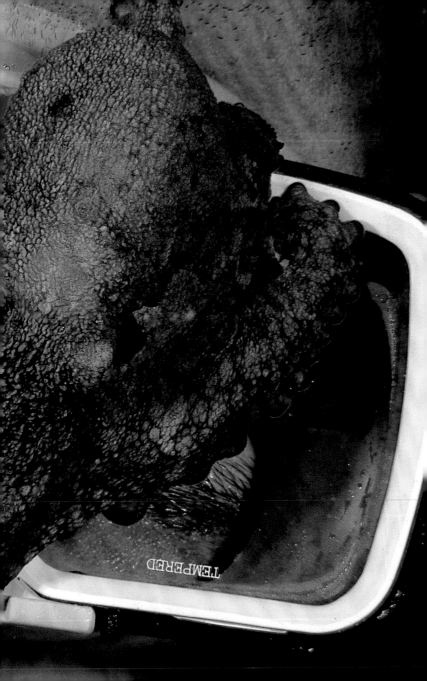

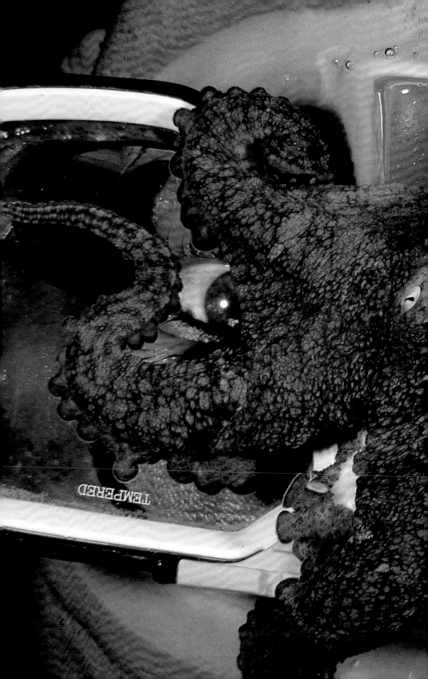

For Jennifer

US photographer David Doubilet has been snorkelling since the age of eight. At thirteen he started taking his first underwater photographs in the green sea off the New Jersey coast and published his first pictures in *National Geographic* in 1972. He is widely acclaimed as one of the world's leading underwater photographers and has reported on most of the world's oceans, covering everything from shipwrecks to sharks. He is a contributing photographer in residence at the National Geographic Society, an honorary fellow of the Royal Photographic Society, and has won many awards including the Lennart Nilsson Award in 2001. His other publications include *Water Light Time* (1999), also published by Phaidon Press.

Index